THE
STORY OF JOB
—A RETELLING

Anita H. Rosenau

To order additional copies of this book, contact:
Xlibris Corporation
1-888-795-4274
www.Xlibris.com
Orders@Xlibris.com
17768

CONTENTS

CHAPTER	PAGE
JOB: 1	1
JOB: 2	6
JOB: 3	9
JOB: 4	12
JOB: 5	15
JOB: 6	18
JOB: 7	22
JOB: 8	25
JOB: 9	28
JOB: 10	32
JOB: 11	34
JOB: 12	37
JOB: 13	40
JOB: 14	43
JOB: 15	46
JOB: 16	49
JOB: 17	52
JOB: 18	54
JOB: 19	57
JOB: 20	60
JOB: 21	63
JOB: 22	67
JOB: 23	71
JOB: 24	73
JOB: 25	76
JOB: 26	77
JOB: 27	79

CHAPTER	PAGE

JOB: 28 82
JOB: 29 85
JOB: 30 88
JOB: 31 92
JOB: 32 96
JOB: 33 99
JOB: 34 103
JOB: 35 108
JOB: 36 111
JOB: 37 115
JOB: 38 118
JOB: 39 122
JOB: 40 125
JOB: 41 128
JOB: 42 131

AUTHOR'S NOTES

In this work, I have attempted to put the story or metaphor of Job into some perspective so it would be appealing to both Bible scholars and those totally unfamiliar with Job's trials. The format consists of rhymed couplets where Job is telling his story. This is my own version of the form, since there are also ten beats to each line; therefore it is conceivable parts of this work could be put to music. Many variations of the rhyme form are used, as the accents fall in various places within the line.

The first two chapters have been condensed. From Chapter Three to the end of the book, most Biblical verses are used. Many different translations of the Bible were consulted; in a number of cases, Job interjects his own thoughts before the beginning of a discourse from one of his friends.

I have always been fascinated with the fundamental spirit of Job himself, and I find it more effective to express a character's inner thoughts within the limits of poetry. When Job is most philosophical, he is also most poetic. I have included herein a few examples of this.

The famous and familiar lines in Chapter 14 now become, "Man that is born of woman is of few and fleeting days, and full of trouble, too! He blossoms as a flower, then is cut down, withers, fleeing as a shadow but of a passing cloud." In the beginning of Chapter 18, from the depths of his dispair, Job says: "Alone, adrift, an alien from time, I know no future. Split from the past, I'm bewildered in the present vacant void. Where can I look now? I'm not overjoyed to hear my friend's rebuke when Bildad notes the following, which I give here in quotes."

Job's questioning in Chapter 23 reads: "Who can know God? Who can understand His being? He's in one mind and none can turn Him, and so intertwined are what His soul desires and how He acts, no one can turn Him from His purpose. Facts I have to prove that He performs the thing appointed for me. What's so threatening is that how many plans He has in store!" The fate of the wicked man in Chapter 27 Job describes in this way: "Terrors will overtake him, put upon by whirlwinds in the night, the east wind's blast will carry him away as he is cast from home and haven: so fate flings on him without redress or pity; as the dim cold edge of darkness falls he would escape—yet battered by a force that has no shape he's buffeted on every side."

Chapter 28 continues Job's observations: "There is a vein somewhere for silver, out of it the metal's mined, and as for gold there is a place to find it, so I'm told. Iron is taken from the earth, and brass is molten from the stone or ore. Alas, men learned to end the darkness, searching to the furthest bound where they may sink anew with mine shaft into the earth, explore its secrets with their light." Job sees his suffering " . . . as the event whereby man is chastened." Then, from the depth of his soul, he exclaims: "But, oh! If there be one angel, messenger, interpreter, none of this need come to pass: he'll intercede this one of a thousand; to man he'll read his uprightness and what right conduct is." Job realizes, too, "Only a fool, a clown, would ask he tailor justice to man's whim. Men of good sense know how to answer Him!"

Job's closing remarks are also something we need to ponder: "So much for history and what occurred, as in a dream to me: what took me past the tragedy of life to find how we are rooted beyond strife, and forces us to meet God, to commune with him. Alas, we pass this w ay too soon!"

Anita H. Rosenau

THE STORY OF JOB —A RETELLING

BY

ANITA H. ROSENAU

JOB: 1

Who speaks to ages past, and those that hence
are still to come? Now let my tale commence,
and I shall introduce myself. My name
is Job, and from the land of Uz: the same

who claims to love both God and all just men;
who lives despising evil, thought or when
expressed. Oh, blessed be God for amplitude
of substance! I am so forced to conclude

of all men in the east, that He assigned
me most prosperity. And thus resigned
I am to wealth of substance—cattle, sheep,
oxen and asses—all worldly goods keep

increasing. Yet beyond this household good,
my sons and daughters! Be it understood
by far the greatest of all earthly joys
are my three daughters and my seven boys.

This story starts upon a certain day
when all my children feasted, in the way
as was their wont. And when the time was past
lest they, by peradventure, had not cast

all glory to our God, then I arose
and to the Lord burnt offerings I chose
to bring, that they from evil be absolved.
This I would ever do, so I resolved.

How inscrutable are the outward signs
of heaven's actions, and whatever binds
man to the brink, the edge, or whim of fate,
along with sorrows they perpetuate!

Unknown to me, at this time Satan came
presenting himself to God. Ask his aim,
it could well be in heaven's atmosphere
to cause doubt on the mind of God. So near

approaches evil feigning at the throne
of good, whose purpose we deny to own.
The unsuspecting fall into a trap
iniquity has sprung. This leaves no scrap

of evidence, unless we are alert
to see the pressure that sin would exert
upon the innocent. So to the eyes
 of God His angels came, and in disguise

was smirking Satan, the Accuser there.
"Where have you come from?" God asked. "Tell me
where."
A grinning Satan said, "From to and fro
upon the earth, patrolling as I go."

My downfall at that moment was God's praise.
The Lord said: "Have you noticed Job? I raise
my voice to say, of all the men on earth
he is the one most perfect. There's no dearth

of righteousness in him. He will avoid
evil in any way it is employed."
The devil scoffed at such a proud remark.
In cynicism tinged with just a spark

of a sarcastic tone he said, "Why not?
Since You delight in him! Have You forgot
the riches he's attained, all at Your hand?
Small wonder that he loves You. But command

to take away his wealth, You'll see him curse
and even to Your face, which is still worse!"
God could not then refuse to take this dare.
"As for Job's capital, I do not care,

you can dispense with all as you see fit.
Just do not harm the man." Then Satan flit
away to act upon this very thing
that, even as I tell it, still must ring

so laden with the ache of memories.
And when they struck, the list of tragedies
compounded so, I barely caught my breath
before the next one came. To cope with death

we first must comprehend what life's about,
and if man chose, of this I have no doubt,
then he can rise above the tempest's blast.
The speech is simple to pronounce, contrast

how very difficult to execute!
Before the terror of God's will, how mute
we stand. For all at once from grace I fell,
although my trip's one Satan did propel.

Sabean raiders out of Sheba drove
all of my oxen herds away; they strove
with and then murdered all my servants, too.
These acts are glimpses of what would ensue.

Enough to lose my people and the herds,
if that were all, but then I caught the words
(another messenger announced the news)
my sheep and herdsmen had been burned! For views

of damage to assess, I had no time.
Too soon another came to tell me I'm
deprived of camels—they're a total loss.
Since bands of Chaldeans had swept across

my whole estate, they left death in their path.
If this were but the sum of all God's wrath!
Now came marauding Babylonians
who brought such slaughter in their caravans.

What next? My children gathered in one place,
the roof fell on them all! Thus in the space
of but a moment's time, a breath, a sigh,
and they are taken from me. Gone. I try

to voice my agony, all I can raise
is numb awareness. I move in a daze,
tear my clothes in grief and fall to the ground;
there speech moves not pain's barrier, this mound

of such intensity. I search for sight
to find the answers that can shed some light
on reason. When the impact will surcease,
I turn to God, to ask for His release.

"Naked I came into this world of Yours,
and so shall I return, for what endures
You give and then You take away. I bless
Your name. What else, I pray, should I confess?"

So tested by the mighty hand of grief
which spanned all I held dear, saw no relief,
I swerved not in my love for God. It grew
as sorrows multiplied themselves anew.

JOB: 2

Again, the angels came before the Lord
and Satan was among them. To record
the dialogue between the two would prove
who holds our destiny, and also who've

within their grasp the elements of fate.
Much they'd discussed before was voiced this date,
except God added, "Job still does hold fast
his utter faith in Me despite the vast

amount of harm that you persuaded me
to do to him, and for no cause." "Really?"
Satan answered stridently, "Just try skin
for skin and you will find, if you begin

to touch his body with disease, he'll damn
Your name and to Your face." "A Pascal lamb
is what you'll make of him! Do as you please,
but only spare his life." If to appease

the devil, why would God agree, consent
to play the game by his rules and relent
to have me struck with such a case of sores
that I was covered head to foot? More's

the pity! Language never can explain
the agony, the torment and the pain.
The aching, throbbing torture was a thing
from which I sought escape, yet from its sting

I found none. Death, I thought, must now be near—
a concept I should welcome without fear.
And when my good wife, speaking but the truth
(whom I have known and loved since from a youth),

said: "Job, if you continue to attempt
this godly pose through such ill luck, contempt
is what I feel. You sit amid a pile
of ashes and calamity, the while

you relish and retain this upright stance.
With all that God has done to you, one glance
can see what you should truly do is curse
your God who brought, for better or for worse,

this evil to your house." This from the one
supposed to be my helpmate! I'm undone.
"Your foolish words are as the heathen speak,
and not what I'd anticipate from meek

and loving lips. My wife, must we expect
but good and pleasant things from God? Reflect,
if God wants to cause evil, that's His right."
Thus through my trial, my tongue is fastened tight.

Three friends arrive to enter in this plot,
who traveled now to Edom. (I forgot
to mention the country where I reside—
a small detail, but nice to know beside.)

Eliphaz, the first and oldest, so wise
this Temanite, you never would surmise
he was a chief of noble birth, a brother
almost in his love. And then another

Bildad, a son of Keturah, Shumite
he is, and Zophar, a Naamathite.
For when they heard the sorrows that were mine
each left his home, and by his own design

did seek to bring me comfort and console
their friend. When they saw the effect this whole
awful turn in my appearance pronounced,
they scarcely recognized me. They announced

first disbelief which changed into despair.
They wailed as if in mourning, on their hair
they sprinkled dust; on their raiment, too, more
to show the depth compassion took, that corridor

where sympathy's sincere. For seven days
and nights they sat with me. In the true ways
of comrades no one spoke a word. Too great
our grief and heaviness of heart its weight!

JOB: 3

And it was I who broke the silence first.
The words slid from my tongue, a dawning burst
that, like a waterfall, the torrent's stream
dropped with a frenzied fury, which might seem

its pent-up drive could only be the source.
I take no pride in these, they but enforce
the long restraint of silence and the swell
of pain; in sense, the agents that dispel

tacit acceptance of the ills of fate.
Their echoes sound the bitterness of hate!
A day's dream gently breaks the stretch of night,
when darkened sky relents, accepts the light

and dawn comes with a timorous embrace
in the awakening of morning's grace.
Its radiance an incandescent glow,
a gleam of promise spread to dazzling show

of shredded color's luminescent blaze;
till all the vestiges of dark, each phase
must disappear. I view the touch of morn
from its first, faint emergence as if born

of time's necessity. Once I was lost
in wonder at the sight. Now my mind's tossed
with thoughts of such far-reaching, deep concern
I tremble in their deluge. How I yearn

for that intangible, a peace of mind
which still eludes me so. I am inclined
to curse the day wherein I first was born.
If it could only perish, and the morn

that follows night wherein I was conceived
would be mere darkness, having naught perceived
by God. Let it be forever shrouded
in the black it claims to own, so clouded

by death's dim-lit shadows that will stain it.
If I could, this night I would ordain it
severed, broke asunder from the year,
a bleak and joyless thing, like a lone tear.

For those who well know how to swear abuse,
let them revile it with a curse profuse!
And then I'd wish to disappear each star
so the night would be no longer stellar.

No more would men see lights to blaze the sky,
or find a place to see the day slip by.
And so through night this punishment should come
because it did not shut (as opium

can put to sleep the senses of the mind)
the womb from which my mother bore me; bind
the fetal growth so it could never spring
to life to see its troubles triumphing.

Why couldn't I have perished when my birth
commenced, to die before I saw the earth?
If I were never suckled as a child
I'd now be sleeping quietly, defiled

not by what kings nor even noblemen
nor wealthy princes, who over again
keep castles filled with treasures, gold and ore
and gems. Hear me as I cry out, implore

I wish to be dead, dead before the sun
shines upon my lowly birth, as one
still-born. Not so for me! Who knows no touch
of life can stay content, assured as much

that when his troubles cease he can find rest,
and hear no more the sound of the oppressed.
The wicked and the weary, rich and poor
alike in death find freedom, they endure

not their own bitterness, but can rejoice.
The slave finds freedom from his master's voice.
Why can they find their liberty who long
for it in death? I tell you it is wrong

the end of life must be the avenue
where man can find relief! Is it not true
God gives the essence of breath, yet this life
is but a mix of hopelessness and strife?

The thing I greatly feared the most is here!
Though I were diligent, trouble drew near
and so for me no rest, no safety's sleep.
I find no answers—all I do is weep.

JOB: 4

The first reply's from Eliphaz who broke
the silence of my sorrowed friends. He spoke:
"If I talk from my heart, will you be grieved?"
For he so understandingly perceived

how in the past to many troubled souls,
how I instructed them throughout the shoals
of their misfortune they must trust in God.
"But you, when trouble strikes, is it not odd

that you appear to faint under the weight
of your adversity? If I berate
you, it's my love that speaks in your defense.
Should God not have your utmost confidence,

hope and trust, too, when these disasters strike?
Will you say God cares not a wit alike
for you, the righteous and the innocent?
But stop and think! Would He wish to torment

them? Have you ever seen them wrongly used?
It's not His wish to punish them till bruised.
But those who do wrong, those who sow deceit,
will reap the downfall that God's love must mete.

They are the ones who perish in the blast
that comes from Him. Why should we stand aghast
at all their wickedness? Though lions roar
and in their youth are fierce, who can ignore

they can be broken and their vigor cut?
When aged and helpless they'll be scattered, but
this truth, given in secret to me, proves
though whispered in my ear still it behooves

we heed the nighttime vision. It may seem
to be unreal, in sleep but like a dream,
yet its spirit speaks. I fear, I tremble,
fright envelops me and I resemble

a shaking man who sees the spirit's ghost
in thought. I quiver till my hair's almost
on end. In the black stillness of the night
a form appears to me; its shape is quite

obscure—a blurred and hazy shadow—dim
but discernible. In the interim
of what seemed moments as time can appear
(yet but a fleeting second to the ear),

so then a voice spoke, low but still succinct.
Although the image was opaque, distinct
its message: 'Can a man, the mortal shell,
be more just than God, his Maker? Oh, tell

who's more pure, more holy than his God? Trust
He puts not in servants, so God must
have put none in His angels. They are charged
with folly, their mistakes when made, enlarged

by God who views them. When He comes to man,
made lowest of them all, it is God's plan
to form him out of dust: a house of clay
that can be crushed to death in the same way

a moth is brushed aside—by morn alive,
at eventide to perish. None survive
with no thought given to what comes to pass.
Their candle of life all snuffed out. Alas!'"

JOB: 5

"And should they call for help, no help is nigh,
no one it seems will answer to their cry.
And to whatever gods they turn, these saints
are deaf to hear their speech or their complaints.

They die in helplessness, these foolish, vexed
that jealousy consume their anger next.
I say those who in their folly turn aside
from God have a short triumph: they abide

in habitations cursed, and their own sons,
like children cheated, are defenseless ones!
Shattered at the gates, turned to a sliver
none comes to their aid, none can deliver

them. Robbed of their harvest or if consumed
their wealth is swallowed up, likely assumed
by stealth. For misery and suffering
are not accidental! No, they both spring

from the seeds sown of sin. Assuredly,
man's born into trouble: I guarantee
as flames of fire soar to their height,
as birds wing aloft and take into flight.

My advice? If I were Job, I should seek
to God, committing my cause to His cheek.
He is so wise, far-seeing are His ways,
and marvelous the things He does. No praise

can fully speak nor number all God's acts;
the rain on earth and floods to fields are facts.
Likewise, the poor and humble He uplifts
them, also those who mourn. It's God who shifts

their sorrow into happiness. But plans
of crafty men are frustrated by hands
that then cannot perform their enterprise,
success eludes them all. As for the wise,

the cunning, they are thwarted in their schemes.
He disappoints these shifty ones as dreams
become mere visions, not reality;
for they will grope as blind who cannot see

and meet but darkness, be it night or day.
(They'll grope at noontime, too, nor will assay
the difference.) And yet God saves the poor
and helpless from the sword, that they endure

no ill from their oppressors. They have hope
these destitute, beyond their ken or scope.
He stills iniquity, breaks it in two,
for justice is God's end and residue.

And joyous is the man whom God corrects!
Spurn not His discipline, for one detects
in it a chastening. The stern rebuke
is meant to prove God's care is not a fluke.

And if God wounds, He tenderly binds up;
for when we're bruised, He heals us from the cup
of sorrow as His hands make whole. In six
distresses will He save; leave Him to fix

the seventh, too; God's power proves this much:
evil has no ability to touch!
So then regard affliction not a curse,
but as a fount of blessings. These disperse

in times of famine safekeeping from death,
or war, or peril of the sword's swift breath.
Those who falsely will accuse and slander
cannot harm you. Why, should you meander

near destruction, need you be so afraid?
No, you can laugh at it, know where your aid
comes from! Or should you happen in the path
of wild beasts of the earth, even their wrath

cannot harm you; you will find your release
from all that's dangerous, you'll be at peace.
Your home will be serene, in its calm state
you will reside apart from sin and wait

for nothing. What could ever be amiss,
or lost or stolen? What shall be the kiss
that seals all good and brings prosperity?
To know your children are the verity

of blessings far too numerous to count,
more than the blades of all grass their amount.
So let Job, whose life's of long duration,
find in a friend's words some consolation.

No harvest comes until the grain is ripe!
When you have stood before death and its stripe,
you'll learn the past's a patient, kind teacher.
For your own good, Job, hear me its preacher."

JOB: 6

To this I must reply: "The tongue finds tune
to speak the words to answer, or too soon
the moment passes. Thus I take my turn
to say what falls upon my heart's concern.

Who weighs my grief and passion of despair,
my sad vexation, horrible nightmare,
or puts in balance this calamity?
Where are the scales to measure what to me

falls hardest? Oh, far heavier the sand
that rims the seashore's edge! How can I stand
in silence at the stark hand of my fate?
Impetuous may be my words of late,

wild and confused, but think what gave them cause.
The poisoned arrows of the Lord, they pause
to find their mark hid well within my breast.
My spirits drink their venom in the test

God's terrors are arrayed against me. When
wild asses bray from lack of grass, what then?
Do not the oxen moan if they've no food?
Give them to eat, and they no longer brood.

How tasteless is one's food cooked without salt.
Is seasoning of life a spice to fault?
Yet this is what my soul abhors, a meat
which I refuse! Oh, God, I do entreat

You, how I long for such a small request!
And the desire I beg is no test
to search Your motive. If You should command
to kill me, let me die beneath Your hand!

I ask for this destruction, to be snatched
away from care and woes and what they've hatched.
Then I'll find succor and assuage my grief.
I'll find comfort despite pain, seek relief

since I have not, in word nor thought, denied
the will of God. Oh, tell me when I've tried
by actions to conceal them. To what length
must I go? Show and prove me where's my strength

that I can wait in patience till I die.
For this unsparing anguish that's mine, why?
Is power's force or potency in bones?
Is flesh of man unfeeling, hard like stones?

If I am helpless, what's to be my aid?
What can I tell my soul, am I afraid
that wisdom, too, is driven from my hope?
I dwell in dark abyss and there I grope.

How I need kindness, the sincerity
of friends who pity the temerity
of one whose faith is shaken! Who forsakes
the fear of the Almighty, who partakes

in the devotion due from those he names
as comrades? Speak and say why you'd play games
with my affection, deal with treachery
and with no provocation accuse me.

My brothers, I'm a brook of diverse streams
that flood in winter ice and snow extremes.
It will run dry and vanish in the hot
of summer from their place, all but forgot.

So you are all as unreliable
to counsel me without a viable
expression of concern. When caravans
from Tema and from Sheba in their spans

of travel stop for water, they find none.
So as their hopes are dashed, those halcyon
days where I sought your comfort now have flown.
They perished in the ghost of the unknown!

What is more gullible than hope confused?
A disappointment lost, before it's used.
You turn in terror and refuse your aid,
but tell me why, what made you so afraid?

What have I asked of you? Your answer, please.
When have I begged of substance from you, squeezed
from your prosperity to meet my needs?
But speak! You see me as a man who pleads

for your response. Did I ever deem
or ask you save from enemies, or dream
that you excuse or spare me with your might?
Plain speech is all I ask. Have I no right?

Say what I have done wrong—if I can know
then I'll be silent, speak not of my woe!
To talk the truth, instead of tip-toeing
around it has much merit. Echoing

right words with grounds is forcible and true.
As for your criticisms, can I view
them either based on reason or on facts?
Though they may argue for reproach, they're acts

unwarranted. Because I cried aloud
to voice my desperation, be not proud
nor quick to say my words are as the wind
that whirls inside a storm, undisciplined.

Would you assail an orphan, dig a pit
and after that would place your friend in it?
Look at me face to face. You think I lie?
Is it not evident how much I try?

I know the difference of right and wrong;
if I have sinned, I'll take you not along;
I also know the voice injustice takes,
and can discern by ear the sound it makes."

JOB: 7

Still I continued in my diatribe.
"Oh, how mankind must struggle, like a bribe
man's life is offered up to misery.
Do I alone ask for a time to see,

to count the days, so long and hard they are?
As if man were a slave, he works so far
yet longing for the day to end, that time
when evening casts its dark and shadowed climb.

The hireling seeks for naught but for his wage,
am I now come to such a pilgrimage?
Months of futility, nights of despair,
this is my portion and the lot I bear.

Even when my head rests on its pillow
I barely wait to rise, yet I still owe
penance to the night. There I lay and toss
and wait the touch of dawn to stretch across

the sky, and pray for morning to release
me that the ordeal of the night may cease!
My flesh that once was proud and smooth and soft
is now a loathsome dry crust, that too oft

is quite broken apart. God, the sight
of it's like worms, pus spilling open blight!
My days are thwarted, endless, all the same.
So does my life fly by, a tiny flame,

a breath, and much swifter than the weaver's
shuttle. To what end? Caught in the fevers
of my hopelessness, so I remember
much of life is like the wind, an ember

that soon blows away. A cloud will vanish
and disperse, and then the eye may banish
from its view what existed from time past.
What once was bliss is now what cannot last.

I knock on silence: nothing, nothing's heard,
when life is over, neither is a word
spoken. And the dying? Gone forever,
not to see house nor family; never

to know the remembrance, nor grace nor wit
that life is all about, nor sum of it.
No longer can I hold my peace, restrain
my mouth from speaking, nor much less contain

my bitterness of soul. The anguish
of my spirit is seen in devilish
distress of mind! I pose a question now:
am I a monster that God will allow

to set a watch on me? If when in sleep
I can forget my misery, He'll keep
tormenting me with nightmares that the dream
appears more the reality, would seem

a vision come to haunt. Should I not choose
to end my life that serves no purpose, use
the sweet caress of death to close its pain?
I loathe and hate my life! Should I remain

in its circumference when all my days
are shadows, like a vapor in some ways,
a vanity that soon will disappear?
And those who still are left, can they come near

to say what is a man? The mortal learns
that only God can magnify! He earns
the curse of persecution as if born
within its time. So morning after morn

as man I'm tested, every moment tried,
I cannot find escape, I must confide.
Where is my solitude? To be alone
is heaven such as I've not lately known.

And if I've sinned, what is the injury
that I can do to God that He should be
the author of my burdens? Why a strike
upon this fragile mortal till he's like

a care upon himself? Why not forgive
whatever I've transgressed, run through the sieve
of pardon and acquit what is offense?
Too soon I shall be dead. When I go hence

to dust must my guilt follow me? Oh, no!
When I lie in my grave, that portico
that seals forever life, I shall not speak.
And all who look for me in vain will seek."

JOB: 8

When friends speak with affection, we consent
to be disposed to hear their whole intent.
So Bildad answered me: here is the tone
of what he uttered, for my friend is prone

to speak his mind. See how with narrow shape
he leaves no distance where I may escape.
"How long do you propose to rant and rave?
These are the ramblings of a man who gave

no thought to meaning, but like winds that blow
you scatter sayings. I have heard their flow,
here's my rebuttal: our loquacity
is only matched by your audacity!

Would God corrupt His judgment to pervert
or misuse justice? Hear what I assert:
your sons have sinned against the Lord. For this
transgressing, like the vice of avarice,

they have been cast aside, victims of fate
and their iniquity. To mitigate
your punishment, if you would plead to God
and beg forgiveness, you might have His nod.

Thus were you pure and upright in your heart,
your innocence would prove to God, impart
prosperity to you and to your home,
like blessings as a coverlet or dome.

Though humble your beginnings, God will send
good and enrich you amply in the end.
If we could question men of bygone age,
or let these generations be our sage,

the wisdom of the past will teach and tell
that man is like a shadow. He may dwell
upon the earth, but of his yesterdays
a transience, an image that conveys

the echo of a distant chime. I quote
this truth, that as the words merge from my throat,
they may have some familiarity—
that is but their peculiarity.

So those who disregard God have no hope!
Can one attach without a cord or rope?
The rushes, can they bloom out in the field?
Without a soil to live in, can they yield?

All grass needs water so that it may thrive.
Just as these living things are kept alive,
so man needs trust in God. If left without,
he is a hypocrite where hope's in doubt—

cut off—for so the sinner perishes.
When God turns from his face, who flourishes?
Those who to God in faith alone are led?
A spider's web is a gossamer thread,

like fragile hopes of those who seek Him not!
What he relies on will collapse, his lot
is desperate; if on his house he'll lean
it shall not stand. That man, I say, is green

before the sun, no plant of vigor, too.
His branches spread across the yard like dew,
his roots entangled in a heap 'mid stones
along a stream. He disappears and owns

no past, for it denies that he was there.
'I have not seen him,' says the voice of air!
What more can he look forward to? That's all!
The godless man must wither, from his fall

come others springing forth upon the earth.
Yet God spurns not the blameless man; his birth
is joy, but evil-doers will receive
no aid, support is nothing they'll achieve.

This God intends—I'm certain of His will—
in fact your mouth with laughter shall He fill!
With mirth a shouting to escape the lips,
where happiness is king, there honey drips.

And those who hate you will be clothed with shame,
for vestments of confusion's all they claim.
Their dwelling places? Tents that pass away,
destroyed as clouds fade on a sunny day."

JOB: 9

I listen to advice, though it be sent
by friends who love me and I know well-meant.
Still I must wrestle with this baffling thought:
if I have never displeased God, why ought

I suffer? Simply stated, that's the gist
of all these arguments, and I've not missed
the inference in them. I am sincere
in answering thus: "Truly I adhere

to what you've said. No man can win his case
against God; He has power to efface
all mortal rights, and if man will contend
with God, he'll find no answer to amend

the argument. A thousand haunting strains
perplex, with no deciphering refrains.
Since God is wise in heart, mighty in strength,
who has successfully gone to the length

of opposition and survived? It's He
who can move mountains, that's no fantasy!
They know it not whom He has overturned
because His anger spoke. Though unconcerned

the earth appears, still God can shake the roots
of it till pillars tremble. Who refutes
that God commands the sun when it should rise,
or stars to shine at night? These He'll apprise.

He spreads the heavens out, treads on the wave
and makes the monsters of the sea behave.
Such are the deeds and the accomplishments
of God! We speak of His omnipotence,

recount as unreachable as wonder
His stout acts. They're marvels without number.
God passes by me the wind whose course
I cannot see, but must by faith endorse.

For who can hinder God, who takes away
the breath of life in death, who'll to Him say,
'What are You doing?' God will not withdraw
His anger, none can stand against His law.

I cannot answer Him, nor can I choose
the words, in vain their reason I would lose.
Though I were righteous (and I know I am),
still I must play the supplicant. A gram

of mercy, that is all I ask. I plead
if He should hear me, if He'd intercede
in my behalf, I faintly would believe
what's happening to me. Can I perceive

if He will hear my cry? God's temper breaks
me, multiplying wounds when He forsakes
me. Will He suffer me to take a breath?
God fills me with a bitterness like death!

For God alone is vigorous and just.
To justify myself before Him, must
my own mouth condemn me? Or even worse,
to say I'm perfect, prove me the perverse?

And if I'm innocent, dare I to think
of it? I am despised, so that I shrink
to contemplate what is my life. A name
says good or evil, are they not the same

to God? The innocent or good He both
destroys; for I'm convinced God is not loath
to laugh when He strikes with calamity
the blameless ones—so it appears to me!

Yet given in the hands of wickedness
the earth revolves. Oh, I swear to confess
God blinds the eyes of judges, so unfair
their rulings, but He does not even care!

How swift my day, its passage like reed-boats
upon the water's edge; how soon it floats
beyond our vision and is drawn away
just as an eagle swoops upon its prey,

so quickly vanish years, to flee in space
of time and disappear without a trace.
And if I should forget all my complaints
against the Lord, so there remain no taints

of sadness, still I fear that sorrow's rim
would be the drowning pool in which I swim.
If I should wash with snow, could I be clean?
The white of purity is not a screen,

for God will plunge me in a muddy ditch;
my clothes will reek of dirt, the likes of which
are horrible to contemplate or see.
They have less filth than what God thinks of me!

So God, not being man, how can I speak?
If I should answer Him, even in meek
repentance, come within His holy gate,
can I find judgment, who will arbitrate?

Is there no one to bring us two to meet,
to lay his hand on both, who can entreat
in my behalf? Would that He took His rod,
I've had enough of the reproach of God,

and lived in terror of His punishment.
Oh, how I long to speak with confident
and dauntless spirit, yet in this extreme
my heart's fears are more real than what they seem!"

JOB: 10

"Oh, how I weary of the tedium
that is my life! My soul's the medium
of discontent. To give free reign to grief,
I speak in bitterness where no relief

comes. Then I say to God, 'Do not condemn
but tell me why You act. What stratagem
prompts this oppression that You should despise
the man You made?' Then, too, I realize

You smile upon the wicked, favoring
them. You're as unjust as men savoring
the eyes of flesh. Speak of eternity
and say if as a mortal man will see,

how You move through my days and weeks and years,
discerning in what space lie all my fears.
You search for my iniquity and guilt
while knowing sin is not the stone I've built

upon. Yet You'd destroy Your handiwork
and for what purpose? Where can reason lurk?
Though I am made of dust, a house of clay,
shall I be brought to dust again? But say

if I am to be poured as milk, or when
cheese has been curdled, whipped. But even then
I have been clothed with skin and flesh and bones—
a life that You ordained—with overtones

of Providence to watch my spirit's flight.
Preserved by love You gave me, was it right
the only purpose hid within Your heart
was to destroy my soul? How can You start

to measure wrong that You will not forgive?
An error found in me will negative
all good—the slightest evil, I'm undone!
Yet if I'm righteous, by comparison

I still must hang my head, so either way
confusion spells my acts and fills my day.
And as a lion's hunted and pursued,
so You, God, stalk me till I am imbued

with fear for my life. Again and again
Your witnesses speak as a regimen
against me. Better to have died at birth
since my life proves to be of little worth!

These few days ere I go to the unknown,
can I not find small comfort that I've sown
some good? Can You spare me one moment's bliss
before my trip across the dark abyss

from which there's no return? Its shadow's death,
where light is darkness, and there is no breath
of dawn. How true its brightest shining ray
is dark as midnight, somber as the day!"

JOB: 11

Cold comfort is as brutal as it's harsh!
Barren of sympathy, it is a marsh
wherein we sink. What could precipitate
the anger of a friend? I meditate

on this, and so the question that I ask,
why then should Zophar take me so to task?
Hear how he claims my innocence a lie,
when this Naamathite will misapply

the course of reason. By what instincts led
he answers me? Listen to what he said:
"A crowd of words, the very multitude
that you have spoken, to these I allude.

Who justifies a man who talks too much?
Who says that speaking guarantees the touch
of virtue? We who listen to your voice—
the babbling, boasting words— have we no choice

but silence? How you tax credulity
with your much speaking, your garrulity!
You think all your opinions are so sound,
so in God's eyes you're pure? Who gives you ground

to claim to know the mind of God? If He
would speak and say just what He thinks, you'd see
the secrets of His wisdom come to pass.
He knows all you have done. The looking glass

through which God sees is clear!. Doubtless your sin
is punished less than you deserve. Begin
to view the mysteries of wisdom: so
can you by searching, find and fathom, know

what are the purposes of Him? How odd,
you're qualified to judge Almighty God!
For His perfection is discernible,
and higher than the heavens, learnable,

yet deeper than the underworld of hell!
And You? Compared to God, you're but a well
run dry of knowledge. So His spirit's sphere
is wider than the earth, and yet so near

and broader than the sea. For who can halt
God? Who imprisons and arraigns, to fault
or much less hinders Him? He knows the vain
and sees their evil, considers the chain

of the guilty and will take note of it.
The challenge is man's, to his benefit.
Your incorrigible stupidity
is more like seeking some validity

that a wild ass's colt were born to man.
But if you'll turn to God, perhaps you can
get understanding. Yet before you do,
put forth your hands toward Him. I caution you,

prepare your heart. For if iniquity
should be found there, then you're in jeopardy,
unless you cast it from your home and pray
it is behind you. Then what dawns? The day

when you can lift your face (a spotless, pure,
clear shining, steadfast ray), and know that you're
without fear and forget the troubled past.
Accept your fate without the conscious blast

at heaven's gate. Then memory shall dim
as waters wash all dirt away, no rim
'round the clean, cloudless sky of noon. A sight
as fresh and fair as morning will be night.

Take courage for you'll then be confident,
lie down in safety, know hope excellent;
secure in God's protection, know no fear
like those who look to you for help, come near

to seek your favor. As for the unwise,
their wickedness pursues them, so their eyes
will fail and they can know of no escape.
Their only hope is death and its dark drape."

JOB: 12

I'll tell what that last sermon meant to me,
those thoughts so filled with inconsistency:
the promise of a better day, if good,
shows no compassion. How misunderstood

I am! He calls God's ways inscrutable,
and yet presumes on the immutable.
So in response, here are the words that slid
from my lips: "How is it wisdom's not hid

from you? Do you know everything? And yet,
there are some things I know and won't forget!
Because you think yourself superior
that makes it so? I'm not inferior

to you. I understand all you have said,
and I, who begged God's help, was even led
to reason with Him who once heard prayers.
Now from my friends all I own is their glares.

Do you believe I'm just and innocent?
Yet how you sneer at me! It's evident,
it is a simple thing to mock and scorn
one who has fallen and who's most forlorn!

When robbers prosper, is justice asleep?
Those who provoke God are secure and keep
all good that God provides. The beasts will teach
and birds will tell, even the earth must preach

this lesson. As for the fish of the sea
they, too, declare the very majesty
of God. So by His hand creation's wrought,
and by His word each living soul is taught.

For God alone breathes life in all who live.
To this wisdom all the lives of men give
proof: thus a man's mind tests what it is told,
just as the ear tries words, how they unfold

the meaning of each utterance, as meat
is tasted by the mouth. Is it discreet
to say all older men are wise? Is length
of days where understanding dwells? True strength

is, does, reside with God alone. He knows
where His dominon lies. His counsel shows
if He pulls down, none tells the Lord to cease.
When He imprisons, there is no release!

When God withholds the waters desert-like
the earth becomes, and with a single strike,
filled with a drought. Yet when He sends the rains
they overrun the land and flood the plains.

Thus power, providence, strength and success
belong to God. It's He alone will bless
the cheater and the one who is deceived.
Are they not both His slaves? How I am grieved

He makes fools out of counselors. Careers
of judges driven mad, so it appears,
are in His hands. And kings become God's pawn!
Since they are bound with girdles that are drawn

about their loins, these bands serve as a mark
dispensed by God, who as the patriarch
grants regal dignity by His own grace.
If it's His wish, He can conceal His face

from us. And even priests are overthrown,
the mighty stripped of power as they are blown,
their ancient orders spoiled. As for the speech
of orators, their voice God will impeach.

Even the understanding of the aged
is lost from them, their judgment disengaged.
Contempt becomes an ointment that is poured
on princes, and their arrogance His sword

will slash. The wisdom of God penetrates
the most profound and hidden, radiates
the dark with floods of light. Even the shades
of death are shadows that God's law persuades!

He will rise up a nation then destroy
its greatness. Short the span left to enjoy
the moments of its dominance, and those
who are the leaders, as a door will close,

so they are barred and this without redress.
They'll wander in a way of wilderness
and stagger without light, grope in the gloom,
no guidance from above, such is their doom."

JOB: 13

"How many instances I've seen and heard
to know what you know, and from them inferred
I am in no way your inferior,
although my life has been the drearier.

How I would love to speak to God, to Him
seek for an explanation of His whim!
I'd gladly argue with Almighty God,
instead of reasoning with men, whose nod

is as fools misinterpreting a theme.
As forgers of lies, doctors who blaspheme,
I beg of you be still and hold your peace.
Let silence be your wisdom, not caprice,

then you can pass for wise men! Hear me now
and to my reasoning, what I avow.
Will you continue to speak wickedly
words God says not, who knows no trickery?

Hear what I say, I who must plead my case
to you who'd take God's part 'gainst my disgrace.
Does God need help from you who twists His acts
with flattery and untruths? God extracts

the reason locked behind the gates of thought
that prompts each deed's performance. So He ought
to understand all motives. What you've said,
shows that His majesty fills not with dread

your heart. Your sayings are proverbs of ash,
and since they are, they count no more than trash.
And your defenses, these I view as clay
that falls and crumbles, as must be the day

of those who curry favor from on High.
Now, silence! If you'd let me alone, try
to form my words in molds, whatever haps
I'll take the consequences, and their traps

though it be death (which I fully expect),
so let my neck be in the noose. Neglect
I cannot to lay my life on the line,
since I but argue for ways that are mine!

Does not the virtue of my readiness
to argue my case prove what I confess?
Once I've disclosed my cause God must acquit,
and I'll be justified. No hypocrite

my God! Now hear again and listen, too,
this is my case, the sum I plead to you:
I know I'm innocent, righteous beside,
I'd argue this point even if I died.

Oh, God, I beg You, spare me but two things,
then I'll not hide my face, for shame it brings:
do not abandon me, forsake me not,
and free me from the terror of my lot.

The awesome dread Your presence holds is such
I cannot answer to Your summons, much
as I should like to do. Tell me what wrong,
what sin I'm guilty of, I'll plunge headlong

to rectify iniquities. So turn
Your face not from me. Oh, God, neither spurn
my plea and view me once again a friend,
treat me not as a foe! I beg You, end

this separation! As a driven leaf
is blown about by wind, its tenure brief,
so who can blame it for the course it takes?
Like chasing useless straws, such action makes

no sense. So are the very things You write
against my name. As You would bring to light
the follies of my youth, to bear close watch
on all my errors, You count every blotch!

I am imprisoned with my feet in stocks,
shut up on every side, no one unlocks
the chains that fetter me. As with decay,
my life's a garment moths have chewed away."

JOB: 14

"Man that is born of woman is of few
and fleeting days, and full of trouble, too!
He blossoms as a flower, then is cut
down, withers, fleeing as a shadow but

of a passing cloud. Viewed with disdain,
You demand accounting, count again
in court a judgment on him. Who can bring
that which is clean out of an unclean thing?

For You to ask from him who's born impure,
a chaste and spotless virtue won't secure
it, since You have allotted to mankind
so brief a span of time in which to find

his being. Numbering his months and days
by limits that You set, an angry gaze
is ever on poor, hapless man. But grant
that he find rest, a short respite, a scant

relief before he dies! A tree can trust
if it should be cut down, through hope it must
yet sprout again. Its tender branches grow
and multiply, although the roots below

are old and parts have fallen to decay;
yet by the scent of water still it may
bud like a seedling. Not so man! When he
dies, buried in the earth till heavens be

no more, that is the end of him. A breath,
a wind, where does his spirit go in death?
So like the waters of a vanished lake,
a river disappears in drought to make

no swift return. When man lies down to sleep
he shall not rise, his passing is to keep.
Oh, that I might be hidden in the grave,
concealed until the wrath of God so gave

way and could be appeased! Appoint a time
when You'll think and remember me, for I'm
persuaded then I need not feel despair.
Yet if man dies, can he return to air?

This thought may give me hope, that I await
till I am changed and my relief comes late.
God calls to me to answer, a reprieve
that my work is approved. What I achieve,

can this be so? Dare I presume to dream
this outcome fits into God's holy scheme?
As it stands now, God keeps a strict account
of every step, watches my sins amount.

Just so my faults are stored as evidence,
sealed in a bag to keep is each offense.
Mountains may wear away, dissolved from sight,
and stones may be dislodged without a fight;

water grinds stone to sand, and torrents wash
the soil away, so God will likewise squash
the hopes of man. Frail man! On him prevails
the might of God, which does not cease nor fails

against him as he passes from the scene.
So man is sent where none will intervene
on his behalf. He shall not know his sons
if they be honored, if esteemed, which ones,

and if they fail, he can't perceive their loss.
How fallen in iniquity across
the rim of sight they are! And so this man
feels pain and sorrow, nothing else he'll scan."

JOB: 15

Thus with the deepest sigh of miseries
I end my speech. The torch of verbal pleas
is taken up anew. This time the end
pursued by Eliphaz, once my staunch friend.

"You are supposed to be a man of sense,
yet speak a foolish tongue with impudence.
To speak with useless words that profit naught,
and serve no useful purpose is well fraught

with danger. What? Have you no fear of God,
no reverence for Him? Only a clod
would let sin tell the mouth what it should say;
deceit becomes your language in a way

condemning you, not I. Were you the first
man born, whose origin stems from the worst?
Hear what the secret counsel of God claims.
Have you a corner on its wisdom, aims?

What do you understand that we know not,
with us are old men, too, have you forgot?
Does not the comfort of your God suffice,
His gentle consolation good advice?

Why should this anger of yours carry off
your heart to vent its passion? Your eyes scoff
when you turn against God; but what are these,
the words you spill in torrents, like a breeze

that whirls around? Now hear this thought I chose,
are you so pure and righteous as you pose?
How do you justify yourself as man?
Why, even God does not reply, nor can

He fully trust His angels. When it comes
to things celestial, even all the sums
of them in purity cannot compare.
How much less man who breathes in sinful air,

and drinks iniquity as a ground swell
of water rises from a sunken well?
Listen, and I will answer from the deep
profundity experience must reap.

As generations have passed on the flame
of learning, so the wise of old proclaim
as they imparted to our fathers this:
the land that God gives without prejudice

is for the family of men alone,
no stranger can sojourn there nor be known.
Throughout his life, one of wicked intent
is plagued by pain, anxiety the bent

that follows him becomes his earthly store.
The sounds of terror to his ears are more
fearsome, they surround him every side,
and even if prosperity abide,

his peace shall be destroyed in plundering.
He dares not brave the darkness wondering
who will accost him. Death becomes a room
to him who fears the sword his final doom.

And so he travels ever in the search
for food to beg his bread; this is his perch
of fear, distress and anguish are his fate.
His enemies (as kings negotiate

a victory) they win every case.
Who argues with God must be in disgrace!
His armor is a tin shield, no defense
against the might of the Almighty; hence

though he may clench his fist defying God,
and stubbornly assail Him, still the rod
of His displeasure finds the fat and rich.
The bloat of wealth can't save these from the ditch

where they must fall. In conquered cities they
dwell, unoccupied and ruined, a prey
to the breath of God. Neither can they keep
the harvest of their gain, nor can they reap

the spoils that they so eagerly attained.
Ah, foolish riches! So is money gained
as vanity. For he who trusts in it
will be deceived, and his reward befit

the hoax of its illusions, as the chime
of falling blossoms drop before their time!
Unfruitful as the withered grape is hope
of the ungodly, a bare lot to cope

with desolation! God's fire consumes
their homes of bribery; likewise their wombs
conceiving mischief, they give birth to woe.
Is not wickedness all their hearts can know?"

JOB: 16

The round of speeches next turn to me, Job.
Here I reiterate my thoughts, disrobe
before my friends, lay bare the realm of mind.
"Have I not heard these words before? What kind

of comforters are you? Shall vain words have
no end? They flow a miserable salve
from foolish tongues. What was earlier said
to give you cause? Perhaps I should be led

like you, if I were also in your place,
heap scorn and shake my head at you. Efface
that logic! No, I should speak in a way
to help you. Why should I wish to repay

you with more grief? With my encouragement
would my condolence flow as streams so sent?
How to defend myself, in silence or
in speech? My grief remains a constant, for

I know not how to turn. A weary soul
I am and desolate. I've lost my whole
family. Look! I'm turned to skin and bones.
A proof of sins, you say? No one who owns

my sorrow would agree. How God must hate
me, tearing at my flesh, intimidate
me with His wrath, to gnash His teeth and snuff
out signs of life until I cry, 'enough.'

The evidence piles high against my case.
My enemies are gathered, and the race
is theirs when God delivers me to them.
The jaws of these false comforters condemn,

they smite me on the cheek, and then they spurn
me. To the hands of sinners, God will turn
me over! He's broken me asunder;
though once I was at ease, now I'm under

His government's regime. An arrow plies
to its target when it hits the mark. Flies
of His archers encompass me, surround
me, and from my wounds blood pours to the ground.

Again and yet again, breach after breach
God makes of my defense; then He will reach
out and attack as giants crush an ant.
God is one warrior who's confident!

And here I sit in sackcloth, having laid
my hope for glory in the dust—I've paid
the price in weeping. See, my face is red
from tears, and blinds around my eyes have spread.

Death's shade is what they portend, yet no wrong
have I done. Innocence I claim along
with prayer that is pure, and violence
is not a trait that I give audience!

Oh, earth, do not conceal my flow of blood,
let it protest in my behalf! No mud
must ever cover up my cry, for now
there're witnesses in heaven telling how

I am unspotted, with a record clear
above reproach. Even the atmosphere
speaks of a witness who will plead my cause.
Though chums disdain, my tears to God won't pause.

I plead that God may listen and take heed,
as one who hearkens to a neighbor's need.
In a few years to come p'rhaps I'll discern
the road all must go down, where none return."

JOB: 17

"And yet that path is here! My days may cease
for I am sick to death. The grave's release
makes ready for me now, and those who mock,
why their offense surrounds me as a lock

holds in a prisoner. So on all sides
I see them with my eye, the snare derides.
Oh, will no one confirm my innocence?
Give me a pledge, cast off your reticence!

For God concealed your hearts, that you know not
nor understand my plight. I beg for what
can keep you all from triumphing. My friends,
are you too prejudiced to make amends?

Denounce your fellowship, accept a bribe,
and let the penalties that I describe
be where your children's sight will disappear,
for God's made me a mockery. I fear

I am as one held up for ridicule,
a target for their jibes, disdained a fool.
The reason for my sorrow dims my eyes,
and I'm a shadow of myself; I prize

what upright men will say when they appraise
how I am changed, and in what diverse ways.
The guiltless ones over the hypocrite
must triumph, and their strong hands shall acquit

the righteous who move on to victory.
The pure in heart grow stronger, this I see.
But you! Come now, renew your argument,
though I expect no new acknowledgment

of reason—who among you is so wise
that you can sit in judgment and chastise?
I fear the good days of my life are past.
My hopes are gone, too—I'm as one harassed.

My heart's passions are broken! Echoes call
how night is day, and day a night dream. All
lie, for they pervert the truth! When I die
the grave becomes my house, and then must I

go out into the darkness, spread my couch
in the dank underworld. For I avouch
that this is where my hopes lie; though I protest,
yet in the dust alone, there is my rest."

JOB: 18

Thus have I ended views of my despair,
sad pessimism pervading the air!
Alone, drift, an alien from time,
I know no future. Split from the past, I'm

bewildered in the present vacant void.
Where can I look now? I'm not overjoyed
to hear my friend's rebuke when Bildad notes
the following, which I give here in quotes.

"How long do we wait till you end these words?
Speak sense for once! The foolishness that girds
your thought precludes our answering. From your
remarks who can assume a sane, mature

response? Why, you treat us more like cattle!
As dumb beasts you view us in your prattle.
You are the one who tears himself in two
with rage and anger. Just because you do,

should this commence an earthquake? Must the world
be unhinged, just because you have been hurled
about in some adversity? Ah, no!
It is the wicked one whose light must flow

away. As the sparks of a flame are spent,
so shall the radiance of his lamp vent
no illumination. As for his stride,
those confident steps narrowed, how they hide

a disobedience that traps his plans.
Then he will see, with failing strength he scans
the net which strangles him in his defeat.
The snare is laid and will become complete

when robbers ambush him. They will prevail,
these terrors that confound him, on a scale
which circles every path he takes. For this
he has good cause to fear. What's more amiss

than that destruction lurks on every side?
Disaster waits for him to stumble, pride
in his firstborn is quenched by hunger's reign;
calamity awaits his wife again

to pounce on him. Disease erodes his skin,
the flesh unsightly where it once had been
so smooth, so death devours him. As by stealth
what he has confidence in most, his wealth,

rejects him as his home must disappear.
With a barrage of brimstone, God makes clear
His wrath. This life is then a tree whose roots
below dry up, its branches bear no fruits.

And the remembrance of him perishes
from all the earth! All that once cherishes
his name shall be forgotten; so driven
from a kingdom of light, he is given

to darkness. Thrust out, banished, he is hurled
even without offspring from out this world.
The day that marks his fate, they of the west
shall be appalled; those in the east obsessed

with horror at his doom. Both young and old
acknowledge this will happen. So we're told
thus fares the godless man where evil dwells.
Those who refuse God live their lives in hells."

JOB: 19

A man reflects upon his life to see
what he will leave to be his legacy.
What could be worse than to leave naught behind?
Perhaps the solace of friends who are blind!

So bitterly I'm forced to answer thus:
"You talk like this, but I am curious
why you persist to vex my soul with speech.
You let your words and thoughts do more than reach

my breaking heart, to crush me with reproach.
Ten times you have said thus: will you encroach
upon our friendship to speak even more?
You say I sin? How odd you come before

me with no shame to deal as strangers would.
For if I have been wrong, the least you could
do is to prove your claim of my disgrace.
If you feel so self-righteous to my face,

then show my guilt. You know how God has thrown
me down and caught me in His net. I groan
with cries concerning violence and wrong,
yet no one hears my cry. I must belong

to those who know no justice; I clamor
for the rights I should not have to stammer
for. God has fenced my path, walled up the way
to block my road, turned off the light of day.

He's stripped me of my glory, cast me down
and from my head He has removed the crown
that once paid honor to my name. My hope
is rooted up, destroyed! How can I cope

with God's wrath which He's kindled so it burns
flame hot? Am I His enemy who turns
His troops against me to surround my tent?
They lay siege at my camp, and won't relent.

He turns acquaintances and brethren, too,
estranges them so all who even knew
me in the past, those whom I befriended,
treat me as a stranger. I depended

on my friends and relatives alike; but
I'm a foreigner to them, cut off, shut
out even from servants who, when I call,
refuse to answer me. I even crawl

and beg, beseech them, yet to no avail.
And worse, I nauseate my wife! I fail
to be recognized by my brothers. If
that were but all! When children get one whiff

of me as I stand to speak, why, they mock.
I am despised, become the laughingstock
of my most intimate friends. Those I love
turn against me, not with a gentle shove,

but with contempt! I am mere mortal bone,
who barely has escaped from death alone.
Oh, my friends, pity me and sympathize;
spare me your mercy, let it neutralize

the persecutions God has willed to touch
me in His anger. So I ask how much
must you extract? Are you still not content
with how I've suffered anguish, the extent

of it? And must I write my plea on stone
forever in a rock till it is known?
Against all, I have a strong conviction
my Redeemer lives, His benediction

is my one hope! So God will manifest
His love at last, when He has reassessed
my character. Then He will stand upon
the earth, a witness who will speak anon

to vindicate me in His court. Though death
may claim my flesh, I know with living breath
I shall see God proclaim my righteousness,
not as a stranger but a friend. I bless

this yearning that I'll find Him on my side,
see Him at last no longer to deride
poor Job! Well my heart fainted when you said
how I brought this upon myself. I bled

to hear you speak, you friends who persecute
as if I'm guilty. I am resolute
before such accusations. You beware,
the sword points equally to you! And where

it points there slander and false charges dwell,
and you're in danger. You cannot dispel
the sword that's poised to judge. What's imminent
comes from God's mighty hand, His punishment."

JOB: 20

Next it was Zophar, the Naamathite,
who thought he had to answer, set aright
my arguments. In haste he spills this thought:
"You've tried to make me feel ashamed, you ought

not to have done so, for your censure brings
an insult, your reproach a shame. It rings
a sound, alerting me to words I know
not where the spirit of them comes, to show

what has been ever since the world began.
Short-lived the triumph of the wicked man!
Alike the happiness of hypocrites
is but a moment, then is crushed to bits.

Though they be proud as heaven, and will walk
with heads above the clouds, this idle talk
means nothing. They will perish like their dirt;
forever cast away, they will exert

no memory, but fade as does a dream.
No one will wonder where they've gone, nor seem
to care. The eye that once beheld these men
will never see the likes of them again!

His children, suffering in poverty,
will beg for bread and know the recipe
for sorrow. By hard labor they'll repay
his debts! And though his age be of a day,

his bones of youthful vigor, still his sin
stays on until the very dust comes in
to cover it. His wickedness appears
as something succulent, its taste adheres

as he will savor it. But soon his food
turns in his stomach, so we must conclude
it is as bitter as the gall of asps.
The riches he has swallowed, now he gasps

on them. His plunder he'll spew forth, expel.
Like poison it will be to him, like hell!
He shall enjoy it not, nor will it give
small comfort or enjoyment. So he'll live

where no streams of honey are. Rivers flow
as does the fruit of his toil—all must go!
He who forsakes the poor, hounds to oppress
these and abandons them, finds his redress

when he'd take what he had no mind to build;
his greed is restless, or at worst self-willed!
Forget what he's attained, it is for naught,
and nothing's left of all the things he's sought.

The fullness of sufficiency's a dream
to him, a brief, gossamer-like moonbeam.
Because he stole, there will be nothing left,
for so he's paid to answer for his theft.

When he would fill his stomach, God will cast
the fury of His wrath upon him fast.
And his food? God's reign of angry ire,
where the weapons of God's arrows fire

to strike him in his body. Like a screw
their gleaming points will pierce completely through
his person! So death's terror, darkness, shall
consume him, and as its blaze whose locale

needs no fanning, so its rage will devour
all he has. All treasures lost! In that hour
heaven will reveal his sins, and earth rise
to testify against him. With his eyes

he'll see his worldly goods evaporate.
Flown far away, they will delineate
the wrath of Him—he waits, with censured nod,
the heritage decreed to him from God."

JOB: 21

This theory, retribution for sin, finds
me totally opposed. I've seen the kinds
who profited from evil, and well know
that good becomes the recompense to flow

to the ungodly. My answer's shuttle
must come forth, and this is my rebuttal:
"Hear diligently, listen to my speech,
and let this be your consolation's reach!

Now I'll tell you of my mind's idea,
though you may mock, deride, if you see a
need to. Yet as for me, if my complaint
were against men (which it is not), I'd paint

another picture. Notwithstanding, why
should not my spirit be impatient? Fie,
upon you! Look at me and be appalled.
Put your hand to your mouth, you who have called

out against me. And when I even think
of circumstance, what forms the missing link,
I tremble terrified. And muttering
I am aghast at my sight, uttering

with horror what I see to be the truth.
The wicked live to a ripe age; in youth
and as they grow, their power multiplies.
Their children flourish in their enterprise,

and their descendants prosper safe from fear.
God will not punish their house nor besmear
it. All their cattle are productively
engaged, no wrath of God destructively

pursuing them. Their happy children sing
and dance, their wealth denies them not a thing!
How they make merry to the sound of flute,
rejoicing with the tambourine and lute;

they wear prosperity throughout their days,
and go in peace to death. A moment's phase
despite the fact they ordered God away,
want not His knowledge and in every way

depart from Him. 'And who is God,' they scoff,
'that we should serve Him, come before his trough
to pray to Him? What profit will it be
to us?' Such the wicked ones' subsidy,

that everything they'll touch will turn to gold.
Not from their hands alone do they behold
success! I have no dealings with this kind,
they are removed from me. Yet bear in mind

so often one says how the sinner's flame
will be snuffed out. His candle burns to shame
the meek! God's anger and destruction come
not to them, they escape without a crumb

of sorrow. So when God distributes ill,
He strips the evildoer of his fill.
You'll find they're driven by the wind like straw,
or by the storm carried away. No flaw

to note this often! If one counters with,
'God punishes their children,' that's a myth!
And I reply, 'The man who sins it's he,
not his sons, who repay iniquity

to drink the wrath of God.' And when he's gone
to pass through death, can his eyes look upon
some pleasures to enjoy? No, for his score
of days and months are measured evermore!

God is a judge supreme. None can reprove
nor teach Him knowledge; no one can remove
His sentence nor decree. To presuppose
your wisdom sets the rules for God, why those

remarks are heresy! His angels still
have to respond, acknowledging His will.
Though one may die robust and hale, in peace
and in security, no comforts cease.

Another dies in bitterness of soul
who never tastes prosperity, the whole
of his life he has known despair. Yet both
are buried in the same dust, no worms loath

to cover them. I know your reasoning
and your opinions; of their seasoning
I've savored, for you'll say to me the rich
and wicked men alike fall in the ditch,

come to disaster's end because of sin.
But I reply, 'The questions you begin
to ask, if you'd speak to an ancient seer,
from this wise one you'd learn this very drear

and dreadful truth: the wicked, evil man
so oft is spared calamity. He can
go scatheless from the wrath of God, who lets
none rebuke him to his face, nor gets

one to repay him for the deeds he's done.
None will pronounce his guilt, not anyone!
He has a stately grave, and when he dies
a great procession escorts his demise

to keep watch on his tomb. Even the dust
of earth is sweet to such a man! So must
success in wickedness in his career
draw others to his way, and thus endear

that course.' So now I'll lay my case to rest
with this, my last remark: put to the test
your arguments fail, for they comfort me
with empty nothings of false charity."

JOB: 22

Another round of speeches will begin,
assert the fallacies their genuine
beliefs belie. How tiresome the threat
of more advice that does not help! And yet,

the newest argument will ever fill
its travels past asserted lies, until
it reaches accusations of a sort.
This claim, a meaning more than mere import,

that I'm a tyrant! Oh, it may be housed
in charming, sweet and lovely words, but roused
against the yearning to be understood
it still eludes me, as it ever would.

So Eliphaz begins the third and last
of his addresses. More than a wild blast
ignoring what I've said, it stands in stark
contrasting hue. I give this long remark

of his as an example of Job's plight,
how he must listen to self-righteous right!
"Can man be of benefit to God or
give Him knowledge? And what is wisdom for?

Is it an asset to God that you're wise
or even righteous? Does He realize
much pleasure? Because your ways are perfect
does He punish you? No! In retrospect

not that you're pious does He bring to trial
your deeds, but because you're an evil, vile
man whose very wickedness is profound.
And do not think I speak lacking good ground!

For instance, you have at some time refused
to lend money to a needy friend, used
usury as a pledge from him and stripped
the needy of their clothing, too. The script

of your iniquities is long: forbid
the thirsty water, to the starving hid
their bread. (Although men of importance gained
the land, the wealthy live all unconstrained.)

Poor widows you dismissed and gave no food,
to orphaned ones no pitied attitude;
you rather did oppress them in harsh ways
and struck defenseless men. Should it amaze

you now there're pitfalls strewn in your behalf,
and sudden terrors are their aftermath?
Your light, a brooding darkness has become,
where waters overflow you till you're numb.

Is God not to be found in heaven's height?
How high the stars are, yet from them the sight
of God, peering out from the topmost star,
proves He knows what takes place, though He's afar.

And then you ask can God judge from the clouds,
or out of utter darkness that enshrouds;
can He see as He walks in heaven's ark
where mists swirl all about Him? I say, mark

well the path of ancient times those who tread
the road in sin, to find their lives instead
are snatched away before their time. Their youth
is an untimely end; they'll see as truth

how life can tumble, on foundations fall.
The torrent of flood waters, like a squall
will overrun them to oblivion.
They are like those who say to God, 'Have done

with us, depart, what can You do for us?'
An impious thought! Hear my strenuous
denial that I should speak with their tongue.
To credit me with that, I'm deeply stung.

No, they forget God is their parenthood,
the source that fills their house with total good;
the righteous and the innocent may laugh,
while wicked ones find scorn their epitaph.

And what remains of them? They bare the scoff
of those who claim their enemies cut off.
Quenched in the flames of fire they're destroyed!
So ends what evil time they have enjoyed.

But if you make your peace with God, acquaint
yourself with Him, there shall be no restraint
where good will come to you. Receive the law,
hear what He speaks, find favor, be in awe

admitting that you erred. Keep in your heart
His sayings and return to God; your part
in this is to renounce iniquity,
then all will be restored. Your poverty

of soul will be replaced; the smile of joy
and such the pleasures you will then enjoy,
if you but give up all your earthly lust.
These count but treasures whose gold turns to dust.

The gold of Ophir, as stones in a brook,
is naught compared to God, yet is mistook
for wealth. Let God, who is Almighty, be
your precious silver and delight; then see

how you can lift your face to God and pray,
for God will hear you and your cause, to pay
your vows and fill your promises. And then?
Whatever you decree will come again,

for so desire becomes your prayer.
The light of heaven's rays shine everywhere
you'll ever go. The proud will be abased,
the humble raised on high and saved to taste

the aid of God: even the island of
the innocent is set free by His love.
The purity of your unspotted hands
will be the cause of heaven's own commands."

JOB: 23

A brooding from the depth of being comes
to question not my friends, but God! The drums
of this march echo in my soul. I yearn
to hear some answers. Everywhere I turn

they are inaudible, so my reply:
"Hear today this bitter complaint that I
make, for under God's heavy hand I groan.
'The punishment exceeds the fault,' I moan.

Oh, that I knew where to find God, I could
come even to His judgment seat! I should
then talk with Him and forthwith state my case;
my mouth, filled with its arguments, will trace

what He will say to me, perhaps acquit
me of my guilt. His wish, more definite,
will be defined. Will He plead and contend
with me, exerting His force and pretend

to overpower me? No, God will hear
and listen with a sympathetic ear,
and give me strength. The righteous may dispute,
but I shall win a pardon absolute

from my Judge, if only I should know where
He is found. How I hunt in vain! I share
the search with sorrow: I look east and west,
forward and backward, north and south my quest

takes me to right and left, still I cannot
perceive nor find Him. I explore each spot,
yet He's not there. Futile, empty, useless
is my whole scrutiny; nevertheless,

He misses naught: He knows the way I take,
the details, how I live are not opaque
to Him. When He tries me it's the fire
that consumes the dross, then I aspire

to become as pure as gold: blameless, clean
and innocent. I've kept God's way, serene
in knowing I have never strayed His path
nor turned aside. What is the aftermath

of God's abuse? Even there I'm not moved
away from His commandments, it behooved
me to enjoy and treasure them more than
my daily food. Who can know God? Who can

understand His being? He's in one mind
and none can turn Him, and so intertwined
are what His soul longs for and how He acts,
no one can turn Him from His purpose. Facts

I have to prove that He performs the thing
appointed for me. What's so threatening
is that how many plans He has in store!
I feel great trembling in God's presence, more

when I consider how these terrors grip
my heart, which has turned soft and faint. The whip
of God is darkness, and its silence thick,
impenetrable as a mystery's trick."

JOB: 24

"Beyond my suffering, the most distress
is that the cause eludes me, no redress
nor opportunity appears. Justice
does not come from God's court, for as dust is

blown away, so is the time for judgment
flown. Why must the godly wait in vain, spent
by searching for His intervening hand?
Look around you at the crimes of man and

see how many go unpunished. I list
here a few: landmarks are removed and missed;
with violence, flocks and feed are taken hence
(and orphans' donkeys, by coincidence);

the widow's ox is taken for a pledge;
the poor and needy are thrust off the edge
and kicked aside and then pushed off the road
as wild donkeys. The desert's their abode;

they go forth to their toil, seeking their prey
to feed them and their children day by day.
A bare amount sustains them, for they reap
and take from fields of wicked men to keep.

At night, clad with no covering, they lie
naked and cold to watch the dark pass by:
wet with the showers of the mountains their
home—for lack of better—caves of rock where

they may huddle. And then, the fatherless
children they'll pluck from their mother's breast, press
the poor to pledge his child before they'll loan
him money. Thus these desolate intone

how they are forced to go about unclad,
naked they do their work. Were that not bad
enough, yet starved they still must carry sheaves,
and be forced to make oil. Yet none achieves

some for himself, treading the grape press, still
no juice to stop their thirst nor praise their skill.
Over the city how the dying weep!
Their cry for help a moaning wail to keep

the soul of wounded men awake, yet God
does not regard their plea. Can it be odd
the wicked will rebel against the light?
Do they not know who are acquainted slight

with what is good and stay not in its path?
For they are murderers who vent their wrath
against the poor and needy, rise at dawn
and then, when darkness falls, who are their pawn?

Awaiting dusk to cover their intent,
these thieves, adulterers, as one lament
no one will see them; so they mask their face
and break into homes where they've marked the place.

They sleep in daytime, unacquainted with
the light. Black night is morn and tainted with
the terrors of the dark to them. Like death,
so they are carried swiftly hence. One breath

and they will disappear cursed by the earth,
none will behold their way nor vineyard's worth.
As drought and heat speedily consume snow,
thus does the grave treat every sinner so!

None will recall him, even his mother
soon will forget him. Worms feed each other
upon him! Thus are the wicked broken
like trees, felled and uprooted—hear spoken

words but take no advantage—ill-treating
the barren and widows, and then cheating
them, too. Yet even so, God will appear
to give the rich power. He'll engineer

to guard their welfare restoring them to life.
When other people die, they'll know no strife.
So God, watching their ways, will then impart
strength and full confidence, courage at heart.

Though they're exalted, time runs out like sand,
in a moment they're gone like the rest. And
as ears of corn are lopped off at the top,
so are they brought low. For who is to stop

this? That's my contention! Who will dispute,
prove me a liar, or who will refute
what I have to say, or claim I am wrong?
Words are my fortress, they're where I belong."

JOB: 25

Discourse, rhetoric and interjection
will give an argument its complexion.
Next it is Bildad's turn as the speaker,
ignoring me, he acts as the seeker

of wisdom. Yet, I refuse to assign
all truth to him—still I claim some is mine!
"What things are with God? Dominion and fear,
dread His authority, awe resting near

Him. Who is it who keeps order on high?
Who numbers His angels that occupy
the heavens? And name but one where God's light
will not shine! How can you assert your right?

Does this make man more justified than God,
or man born of a woman clean? You nod
your head, you presumptuous fool, who would boast
to understand the glory of God. Most

agree even the circling orb of moon
is less than nothing, nor can it impugn
God's wisdom, so are less than pure the stars
in the eyes of God. If they express scars,

then how much lower can man be? A worm,
a lowly maggot that knows but to squirm?
The son of man is mortal as a leech,
when he's reduced to size, it's meant to teach."

JOB: 26

No more can silence utter nor preempt
the course of my emotions and contempt!
I now must chide my friends who do not solve
the problems I possess, nor words dissolve

them. "What assistance you afford a friend!
Oh, what great helpers you've become! No end
of aid to one who's lost his power. How
do you save the arm who needs his strength? Now

that you've counseled me who has no wisdom,
declaring my stupidity is come,
who assisted you to have so observed,
and who noted it was I who deserved

this? Oh, tell me what spirit is expressed
in you, to speak to one who's so depressed
in soul! How naked is the nether world
where cloak of shadows writhe with fears unfurled.

The waters of the deep and all that live
therein, they tremble that destructions give
no covering. To God, so are the dead
called into being from that watershed.

Who stretched out heaven over empty space,
suspended earth on nothing? Void of grace,
He bound the waters in His thickened clouds
so they'll not burst, held by the mass of shrouds.

Who wrapped the moon's face with a cirrus haze,
to keep His throne concealed from mortal's gaze?
So God has compassed waters in their bounds;
His circle is a boundary of grounds

to separate the day and light from dark.
The pillars of His heaven, trembling, mark
astonishment at His rebuke. The sea
grows calm divided by His power. We

who are the proud, He crushes by His ken;
by God's breath are the heavens made fair when
His hand it is that strikes the serpent's flight.
The swiftly gliding monster He'll requite.

Lo, these are but dimensions of His ways!
Small like a whisper we can hear, and days
know but a portion. Who can understand
His might, His majesty, His thunder's hand?"

JOB: 27

"Why must my culpability be proved?
I swear to God Almighty, who's removed
His justice from me, and my right denied
and filled my soul with bitterness beside.

As long as my two nostrils know their breath,
my lips will speak no lies; no shibboleth
my tongue will utter, no evil deceit
for I shall never say you're right. I greet

that thought with, 'God forbid!' Until I die,
I'll hold unflinchingly my claim that I
am innocent. My life's integrity
proves I need not reproach myself, you'll see

this in all I do. Those who otherwise
would say are wicked men, whose very eyes
have blinded them with evil. What's the hope
of hypocrites? How can the godless cope

if God will cut them off? What have they gained
when God demands their soul for their profane
and sinful ways? And will He hear their call
when troubles strike, distress and woes befall?

Will the sinless take delight in God, pale
at what He does all times? I reach the scale
of what concerns God's hand. This I do need
and cannot conceal it. So I'll succeed

because you, too, have seen yourselves. Again,
why must you be so altogether vain?
This is the portion of a wicked man:
bestowed on tyrants, fate's oppressors can

expect that if his children will increase,
it is but for the sword. They will not cease
to search for bread and miss. Those who survive,
the pestilence will bury them alive.

Even his widow shall not mourn nor weep!
With silver, as if dust were stored, he'll keep
the tarnish of his money as a thing
more certain than his own imagining.

And as for raiment, though he'll think to pile
it on as clay, he will not wear it. While
the innocent divides his wealth, his home
will be frail as a spider's web—or foam

that rises from the sea—a watchman's booth
as flimsy for a shelter, and in truth
as a bird's nest. He'll lie down rich one day,
but not again. His wealth is blown away,

and when his eyes are opened all is gone.
Terrors will overtake him, put upon
by whirlwinds in the night, the east wind's blast
will carry him away and he is cast

from home and haven: so fate flings on him
without redress or pity. As the dim
cold edge of darkness falls he would escape—
yet battered by a force that has no shape

he's buffeted on every side. The slap
of those who openly deride, who clap
their hands with God he feels, and he will see
them hiss and boo him to eternity!"

JOB: 28

Then I continued my defying tone,
the words cascading, my unsparing own,
their source a depth of passion's puzzled doubt:
"There is a vein somewhere for silver, out

of it the metal's mined, and as for gold
there is a place to find it, so I'm told.
Iron is taken from the earth, and brass
is molten from the stone or ore. Alas,

men learned to end the darkness, searching to
the furthest bound where they will seek anew
with mine shaft sunk into the earth, explore
its secrets with their light. And even more

into the black rock shadow's pithy gloom,
they'll look for stones as they are taught, exhume
all from the darkness. Their descent on ropes
will be to swing between the narrow slopes.

And so does the technique achieve its end!
The genius of man's intellect's a blend
of human and divine. So comes a crop
whose harvest is reaped from the earth on top.

Below, turned under as if on fire
they find, raked in dirt, how to acquire:
both stones of sapphires, the dust of gold,
all treasures that no bird of prey can hold,

nor eagle's eye observe, nor have proud beasts
once trodden it, nor serpents find their feasts.
So man puts forth his hand, the flinty rock
he overturns, and mountains he'll unlock

and cut out rivers in between the stone.
His eye seeks every precious thing to own.
He keeps the streams from flooding over, too,
and what is hid he brings that into view.

Yet I ask of you where is wisdom found,
in heaven's sky or deep within earth's ground?
Where is the place of understanding kept?
For man knows not the price, he is inept

to find this even in the living's land.
The deep says, 'Not in me.' The ocean's grand
enormous span says, 'Not with me.' It can't
be gotten for gold, nor significant

amount of silver can be weighed for it.
The value of the gold of Ophir, bit
by bit, or prized onyx, sapphires, too,
can't be compared, nor can one find a clue

that gold and crystal share on equal par.
They cannot be exchanged at rates that are
commensurate with jewels of finest gold;
no mention can be made, a thousand-fold,

of coral nor of pearls. Even beyond
the price of rubies, wisdom is a fond
imponderable! The topaz that comes
from Ethiopia is but vacuums

compared to just one parcel's intellect.
Such is the value of gold you'd expect
to find, and so now I reiterate
my question to you three, all literate

men: can you not tell me where wisdom's traced
and understanding found? And who has placed
the scales to weigh it? For no creature yet
on earth can see it. Even winged birds fret

they cannot find its way. 'We've heard its name,'
death and destruction say, 'know of its fame.'
But God knows both its place and where the path
of wisdom winds. He sees all the earth hath

and everything in heaven, all its ends.
He gives the wind its weight and He defends
His measure of the waters of the deep.
By His decree it rains, and God will keep

the way of lightning and of thunder. Still,
He sees, prepares and declares this His will
and says to man, 'Behold, fear of the Lord
is still the only wisdom to afford.'

An attribute of God! So to depart
from evil is the master of the heart.
True knowledge is to find God the one source,
revere Him and shun evil. But of course!"

JOB: 29

A man, at any moment in his life,
can look behind him, view the good or strife
that is a part of his experience.
And what is past, it makes no difference

if in the present he can have some trust,
for hope is what life teaches—that's a must!
So I continue to speak words that give,
within the framework of comparative

emotion, first a record as if they,
with wings, could take me somewhere far away.
"Oh, that I were as I've been in months past,
when God preserved me, when His candle cast

its light upon my head! When by its shine
I walked through darkness, knowing what was mine.
Would I could be as in days of my prime,
to have God's friendship, know it all the time

about my home; would I could find the glow
of His sheltering confidence, to know
my children's love surrounding me. Oh then,
oh, how I prospered! Would I taste again

the milk of my farms, paths washed with butter,
to see rock streams where oil's poured, to utter
the soft, sweet sounds of success. Through the gate
of the city, as I went out, all would wait

to prepare my place with the elders. Young
men would see me and hide, but those among
the aged would arise and stand with respect.
Princes kept quiet, hands to their mouths, checked

to keep them from speaking; nobles were hushed
and all their voices both silenced and crushed.
The ear that heard blessed, what eye saw approved,
for I delivered the poor and was moved

by all the cries of the fatherless. Yea,
for them with none to help them, I would pay.
Those who were ready to perish they blessed
me, and from their hearts the widows addressed

me with songs of thanks and shouts of pure joy.
When I wore righteousness, none could destroy
the cloak of my charity; all I did
was just and honest, not a thing was hid.

I was eyes to the blind, feet to the lame,
father to the poor. So it was my aim
that even strangers, whom I didn't know,
received a fair trial at my hand. Although

I broke the jaws of the wicked, my plan
made all their spoils to be pulled from each man.
I said to myself: 'I'll die in my nest,
my days, increased as the sand, will attest

the good of my life. My roots are outstretched
to reach their water's edge, while dew hangs etched
on all my branches. My glory is fresh
in me, my bow ever new in my flesh

with the honors that fall to me. Renewed
are my abilities, so I'm endued
with the comfort of ease.' When my words fell
men heard, waited my counsel to tell

what they should do. Then, once I had spoken
they'd wait for more—their silence unbroken—
wait, as the rain is expected. Advice,
once I'd given it, need not be said twice!

For the discouraged, I smiled on their fears,
the light of my clear face canceled their tears.
And I chose the way, I sat as a king
for his army who dulls their suffering."

JOB: 30

"Such was my past, a true natural guide
and comfort to men. But now! Oh, how wide
apart I am from the role I once played!
Now I'm laughed to scorn, derided, arrayed

with the vestige of ridicule. How youth
disdains me by acts far worse than uncouth!
How they make sport of me, those who are sons
of fathers worth less than my dogs! These ones,

what can I gain from the strength of their hand?
Their vigor is vanished; age, as a strand,
moves with the passage of wind; they are gaunt
with famine, the desolate ground will haunt

them. Waste places of the desert they'll gnaw,
pick mallow and the leaves of bushes raw,
and to warn themselves the roots of the broom,
driven out from among men, yet to whom

shouts of jeering are tossed as to a thief.
And their dwellings? Where do they find relief?
They must live in ravines, in rocks or caves,
and among the bushes they'll bray, these knaves.

Huddling together, these children of fools,
of base men more vile than the earth, who rules
this senseless and disreputable brood?
They've been beaten and routed. Like these crude

ones I've become the object of their song—
I'm like a byword to them. All that's wrong
in them they see in me, their loathing fills
the air, they keep aloof. A hate that chills

to such degree, they spit upon my face.
Oh, God, You afflict me with Your disgrace!
You've loosed my cord and bridle, humbled me
and even placed my life in jeopardy.

These now have no restraint to cast me off.
The rabble rise to drive me in the trough
of their destructive ways. To right or
left they mar my path. And if a visitor

should see how they promote misfortune's role
against me, he would be chagrined, console
me for the suffering and grief I bear—
a stranger from some foreign place who'd care!

For so they come upon me through a breach,
so wide amid the crush of water's reach
that rolls upon me. Now, desolation
turned to terror becomes the equation

of my being. My soul, my honor as
the wind do they pursue, as a cloud has
prosperity been blown away. Oh, how
my soul pours out within, and I avow

my broken heart has met with sorrow's pain!
Depressions haunt my days, become a chain;
even my bones at night are racked, the sting
and smart that gnaw them take no rest. A thing

of violence and great force my disease,
a garment meant to bind, I feel its squeeze.
God has cast me in the mire. As dust
have I become, the ashes of His trust!

I cry to Him, He'll not answer nor heed
my call. He's become cruel to me, decreed
His hand against me with great might. He'll lift
me on the wind to ride it, yet the rift

between us grows. Into the whirlwind's storm
I'm tossed! My dissolution He'll perform
to bring me nearer death, which is the house
appointed for all living. So He'll douse

me in the tempest of His anger's whim.
Yet from the ruin's heap I cry to Him!
Did I not weep for those whom trouble struck?
My soul grieved for the poor, for their ill-luck,

yet when I looked for good, then evil came.
Though I'd wait for the light, yet in my shame
a darkness fell. My heart is restless, too,
waves of affliction come on me anew.

I go in mourning blackened not by sun,
I stand up in assemblies, have begun
my cry for help. My weeping is a howl
of jackals to whom I'm a kin. The owl

I do consider my companion. Oh,
my skin is blackened and my bones burned so!
My harp is turned to mourning and my voice
once full of gladness, now has but one choice.

My flute's become the sound of those who weep
the sad lament of sorrow that's to keep.
So I experience the change of tune
such haunting echoes of despair I croon."

JOB: 31

"I've made a covenant that with my eyes
I shall not look upon a maid; surmise
then what calamity the Lord will send
on those who do. They suffer to amend

their ways these workers of iniquity,
for God will measure as He does to me,
and count their steps. If I have walked a false,
vain road, my foot speeds to deceit and halts

not. Let me be weighed in a just balance,
see if I'm innocent, rate my talents.
If I have turned aside, lied or deceived,
if my heart lusts for what it's not received,

or if I'm guilty of some other sin,
I'll sow and let another one begin
to reap the benefits. Even my own
to be uprooted, and before they're grown!

If in my heart I have been so enticed
by any woman, punishment sufficed
and I should die. Or if I've lain in wait
upon my neighbor's door, eradicate

my good, let my wife do the work of slaves.
That would be a heinous crime, no waves
of punishment could pay nor recompense
by judges. Fires of such consequence,

their devastation would destroy to hell,
and burn the root of my increase as well.
Or take another incident: by chance
if I despised my servants, gave no glance

to their pleas when they offered a complaint,
what should I do then when God will acquaint
me with His anger? I'd be bound to ask
what may I say as He takes me to task?

Did He not make us all, create the womb
and fashion each of us with His perfume?
If I held the poor from his desire,
or made eyes of widows fail—inquire

if I have—or withheld from hungry lips
food for the orphans, then I'd come to grips
and understand why I'm tormented thus.
But never have I done these things. Discuss

with me, how from my youth I cared for these
as if I were their father. See, the keys
that will unlock my sympathy are here
within my heart. Let's cite another fear:

if I've seen any perish from his lack
of clothing, and put nothing on his back—
fleece from my sheep, at least—to keep him warm
until he'd bless me for acts I perform.

If I have lifted up my hand against
the fatherless, because I thought or sensed
the verdict would be mine; if I so failed,
then let my punishment be likewise scaled,

and let my arm fall from my shoulder blade,
let it be broken from its socket, made
useless! Oh, how I dread the punishment
of God! The thought of His admonishment

acts like a check. Still more His majesty
keeps me from sinning—it's my remedy.
Again, if I made gold my hope and trust,
or put my confidence in it, I must

have then rejoiced because my wealth was great,
and I possessed much in my whole estate.
Or, if I worshipped as the heathen do
the shining sun, the moonlit glow, and grew

secretly enticed in my heart, these are
sins to be punished as irregular
by judges. I then would be false to God,
denying both His heaven and His rod.

Or, if I rejoiced to see the ruin
of my foes, accept what evil grew in
their ways, I'd still not let my tongue so curse
to ask for their lives—that's a sin, or worse—

and I'm above such immorality!
Would any of my servants now agree
that I deprived them of their food or meat?
Did I permit a stranger from the street

to stay with me? Yes, I made him a guest
in my home, and my doors, at my behest,
were ever open. My deficiencies
I never hid, nor my poor frailties.

Nor have I feared the multitudes and held
contempt for families. Scared and repelled
by those who frightened me, so I kept still
and would not venture out of doors until

I found one to hear my plea. Oh, behold
my desire that God will hear when told
I'm innocent! I pray but have a look
at what is writ against me. Where's the book

of charges, the indictment in my case?
Conscious of my integrity, I place
my head high on my shoulders. As a crown,
I'll wear the charge against me, handed down

where I can find it. At that time I'll give
account of all my steps, how I must live,
present my clear defense and I'll not wince
to set the record straight. So as a prince

shall I approach His throne. One afterthought
that just occurred to me: have I done aught
that my land should cry out and then accuse
me that I stole its fruit? If I should use

that which I did not earn or murder those
who owned the land to claim it, I suppose
as mine if such I ever did, then let
me pay the penalty as judgment's debt.

Let thistle grow instead of wheat, and weeds,
foul weeds, instead of barley grow. Who needs
to add that in the world where I abide
I have been faithful? I have naught to hide."

JOB: 32

Thus ended the third round of this debate
where I insisted, nor would abdicate
from my position of a conscience clear
and spotless. My three friends would never hear

another word I'd say, nor would they speak
again. Not for the reason they were meek,
but they despaired to listen anymore
to pleas of righteousness such as I swore.

Now let me introduce another man,
his name's Elihu, a kindred of Ram,
Barachel's son, a Buzite, who was there
waiting with silent patience to declare

the longest speech that I must listen to.
And I've recorded it, don't misconstrue
my purpose, so another point is made,
one none the others saw, nor were afraid

to say. When he arrives to reach that peak
I'll mark the text, now let Elihu speak.
"My wrath is kindled as a fire flames
and sparks the ashes of burnt wood. The names

all come into my mind as I recall
how you would justify yourself, 'mid all
the clamor of the arguments of friends.
You prove yourself a virtue that extends

beyond the goodness that is God's. I could
not hear all these remarks, though understood
full well, and keep my tongue. My wrath's against
these three who likewise heard but never sensed

where and how to answer Job. They condemned
him, nevertheless! My reticence has stemmed
from deference to age. For I am young,
and you, you all are old. And so I hung

back, more afraid to speak. Yet, when I saw
no answer coming forth, I had to draw
the one conclusion—now my time has come.
I said, more to myself, 'Let days speak some,

and multitude of years teach and expound
their wisdom.' I approach with this profound
appeal: what but the spirit of God can,
the spirit that's almighty, be in man?

What gives man understanding? It is not
the number of one's years that count a lot.
The old are not so altogether wise,
unless it's in their ego-seeking eyes!

The aged are not alone to know what's right;
therefore I say but hearken to the light,
and listen to my thoughts that I express;
I waited for your words, seen them progress,

as I gave ear to reasons while you searched
out what to say. Your arguments besmirched
poor Job! Yet none convinced him he is wrong.
You never proved where must his sin belong.

Beware! Can you say you've found wisdom? No,
it's God, not man, who thrust him down. I know!
Job's not directed words to me; therefore
I cannot respond as you whose speeches pour

but not with logic. Here you sit dismayed,
and find no right reply. Your words glissade,
escape in silence now. Am I to wait
because you can no longer speak? Too late

for that! No, I will answer and declare
my own opinions. What I know, I dare
to say. So like a torrent I am full
of words, the spirit in me visible

to urge me on. My heart is like fresh wine
which has not been opened, so thoughts of mine
are as new bottles, poised about to burst.
I speak but to find comfort from their thirst.

I will show favor to no man, to none
will I use flattery. If I'd begun
to do so, God would put me far away,
and make an end of Elihu today"

JOB: 33

While up to now this youth spoke to us all,
next he addressed, so far as I recall,
what he would say to me. Continuing
to reassert his right to speak, the string

of sentences flowed gushing forth. "Come, now,"
so he commenced, "I'd have you listen how
I say and with what words. My mouth speaks out,
speaks with sincerity, will see no drought

of truth. My heart assures me this is fact,
my lips shall utter knowledge to attract
attention. Since the spirit of God formed
me, and the breath of the Almighty swarmed

into my life, if you can answer me,
I pray you will not hesitate, but see
and take your stand. Behold, I am as you
before God. Made from the same clay, I view

my being as your counterpart. No fear
should terrify you then, nor it appear
a pressure heavy on your soul. To face
a man who's like yourself does not embrace

the same as if you spoke to God! You've had
your say which I have heard. Nothing's to add
to it. Your words repeat: 'I'm innocent,
free from offense, guiltless and confident,

ultimately to be found without blame.
Yet God finds the occasion that would claim
to put me in the wrong. An enemy
is how God looks and scrutinizes me;

to put my feet in stocks and mark the path
of all I do, I'm humbled by His wrath.'
Well, here's my answer, and you all are wrong!
God's far greater than mortals and more strong.

His acts should not be questioned by mere man,
yet you contend with Him, fight all you can
to say He has no answer. To your word
He need give no account—it is absurd

you think He should! So God speaks once, yes twice,
but man perceives it not! Does it suffice
He speaks in dreams, those visions of the night
when deep sleep falls on man, who's bound up tight

in slumber on his bed? It's God who makes
men hear, opens their ear to listen, takes
the course of His instruction to impress
their minds, to terrify with warning's stress.

His aim's to draw man from his purpose, keep
him from pride's way, so that his soul may leap
from out the pit or from life perishing
via the sword. So again, suffering

is the event whereby man is chastened.
The pain on his bed is sometimes hastened
with continual strife in his bones; then
he loses taste for bread, his soul even

abhors the daintiest of food. Like skin
and bones he becomes, so thin he's akin
to a skeleton, flesh wasted away.
His soul draws near to death, to those who'd slay

him down. But oh! If there be only one
angel, messenger, interpreter, none
of this need come to pass: he'll intercede
this one of a thousand; to man he'll read

his uprightness and what right conduct is.
With this God then declares He has found his
ransom. Being gracious, He shows pity,
says, 'Man need not go to the pit.' Pretty

soon the ransom, man's atonement, is seen
in a profound change that can only mean
the pardon of God—man's skin's now fresher
than a child's. He will return to treasure

the days of his youth. When he prays to God,
this God accepts; he also has His nod
and comes into God's presence filled with joy.
The past's a memory God will destroy.

He will recount the way salvation came,
to sing before men of God's holy name.
He'll say, 'I sinned, perverted what was right,
no profit there! But God does not requite

evil for evil. He redeems my soul
from going to the pit of death. The whole
of my life is now a light to see!' Yes,
God does all these things and works His largess

twice, three times. His purpose? To chastise man.
The use of evil in this life it can
bring vindication, so the soul returns
from going to the pit, and then man earns

the right to know. And why? Now, listen well
oh, Job, and hearken to me; I will tell
while you keep silence for I truly speak;
if you have any words then answer, seek

for your reply. For my one desire
is to justify you, know I admire
you and speak the truth. Can you prove what's come?
If not, be still and I'll teach you wisdom."

JOB: 34

The ego of Elihu is a stream
of rippling outbursts, twisting as a dream;
it pauses once to catch its breath, then shifts
direction with the speed of sound. What drifts

the path of his direction, this man who talks
incessantly: the kind who never balks
to raise himself up, putting others down;
who seeks the throne of God as if His crown

already were bestowed on him! I hear
the speaking, the sound of his voice. No cheer
to hear, yet still I am polite. I know
what course he takes, the way his mind will go.

Addressing everyone, so he drones on:
"Hear now, you wise men, and the woebegone,
give ear to me, you of experience.
(Note how he flatters. That's intelligence.)

For how the ear tests, proves, the spoken word
as does the mouth taste meat. We chose what's heard
and eaten, let us then select for us
what judgment is, and we'll also discuss

what good is, too. For Job's already said,
'I'm innocent. I've been unfairly bled.
Deprived of justice, God has falsified
my case, my state is desperate beside.

God thinks I lie. My punishment's severe,
though I have never sinned.' Who could come near
the arrogance of Job? This man drinks scorn
and blasphemy as water! How he's shorn

of reverence. He goes in league with those
who work iniquity and wrong, who chose
the path of evil men. Did Job not say,
'No profit in delighting God, no way

to find His favor?' Now hear, you wise and
men of sense, for surely you know firsthand
God does not practice wickedness, nor do
wrong nor sin. He'd rather (according to

one's iniquity) just punish man, see
that he gets what his conduct deserves. Please
note this with care: God does no evil deed,
is never wicked nor unjust. His creed

is on the earth. And does He not disperse
His heart and hand on all the universe?
If He took back His spirit to Himself
and gathered in His breath, life in itself

would disappear. Why, all flesh would perish:
man, returned again to dust, could cherish
nothing. Do you wish to understand? Then
hear my words. Can it be possible, when

you reflect on it, that God who governs
can hate justice? And who is he who yearns
to condemn God, the one Almighty Judge?
Does He not tell kings they are worthless, nudge

the princes to admit their wickedness?
He shows no favor to the great, the stress
of God is on the rich and poor alike.
They are all fashioned by His hand, the strike

of power that's God's is an awesome sound!
Yet in a one moment all will die; though crowned
with greatness, in the middle of the night,
all these shall pass away before the light

of dawn. They're gone! They disappear. No trace!
Swept from the earth, the low and mighty face
the same predicament. His eye is on
the ways of man. The bad and paragon

of good find that He knows what steps they take.
No darkness nor the shades of death can make
a place where they, the evil ones, can hide.
And no time is appointed when the pride

of men will come before His Judgment Seat.
The mighty men are shattered. He will greet
them with the knowledge that He sees and knows
what happens. So without a trial, He goes

and leaves their spot to others. He'll observe
them in the night, destroy their last reserve,
and overturn them till they are destroyed.
In but a single night He has employed

to crush them for their wicked sins before
an audience of men. And He'll ignore
that they have turned aside from following
His way, so then the poor who cry can bring

their cause to His attention. Yes, He hears
the cry of the afflicted! To His ears
has come the wail of the oppressed. And yet,
if God be quiet, who'll condemn? No debt

must God pay to explain His acts! Say who,
if God will chose to hide His face, can view
it? Both a nation and a man must yield
unable to find fault. For God will wield

His might that no ungodly man can reign.
The hypocrite beguiles, but can his chain
snare any of the people? Who acquits
that they should say to God: 'What benefits

from chastening, we've earned the discipline,
and will offend no more, no longer sin?'
What I see not myself, this God will teach.
If I have done unjustly, then my reach

will not exceed the point. God's recompense
is not as man requests, but impudence
would make a man reject it. Who will choose
the terms? Let Job declare what he knows, use

the words, not I! And will Job now lay down
demands to God? Only a fool, a clown
would ask he tailor justice to man's whim.
Men of good sense know how to answer him.

Job speaks with a wide disregard for truth.
His knowledge is unsure, likewise uncouth,
his words are void of wisdom. Then must Job
be continually tried, wear the robe

of the accused for his sinful remarks
that multiply against God. Who embarks
on such a course has named his strategy:
rebellion, arrogance, and blasphemy."

JOB: 35

These are harsh words a man lays claim to which,
when sorted out, we see what kind of niche
Elihu plans. He does not say, as friends
already have, the fact that he contends:

just this, that omnipotence can do no wrong.
Yet this point must be proved. Life does belong
to God, and He sustains man; this will serve
God's purpose, but the hard facts to preserve

show human misery comes not from out
of God's benevolence. If there's a doubt
to whether there are other facets here,
interpretations will soon make them clear.

Two issues now concern what he says next,
that weave a pattern throughout his whole text:
the one concerns man's inability
to affect God; the other claims, you'll see,

that God is ever independent of
the world of men. His majesty above
insures God's justice. Oh, let him who'll speak
continue in the vein he has! A peek

prepares for his long diatribe, to tell
in his own words the thoughts that flow too well:
how he directly answers what I charged,
the just have no advantage. He enlarged

upon this, though. "Do you think it is right
or a sound plea for you to claim or cite
you are more just than God? For you now call
yourself more righteous, and then ask if all

is lost because you have not sinned, then add
you are no better off than if you had!
I'll answer all of you. Look at the sky,
consider as you look to heaven, try

to think while rain clouds tower over you,
how can your sinning injure God? It's true!
How can it touch Him if you've multiplied
transgressions? Or take your innocence; hide

good and see if great gifts come to God. But
what can He receive from you? How clear cut
your wickedness can reach another man,
and your good deeds profit Him. If they can,

because of your conduct, it's man's concern
alone, not God's. Permit me to return
to make a point: because of many woes,
the people cry and call for help; who knows

if it's by reason of the mighty strength
the rich possess? Yet none will say at length:
'Where is God, my Maker? Where's He who gives
songs in the night; who teaches more, who lives

to make us wiser than the beasts and fowls?'
They cry, but have no answer. Why? The scowls
of evil men cause pride. God will not hear
of vanity, He knows it not. His sphere

is to see all. However much you say,
God notices no man. You disobey,
then must be humbled in His presence, till
your trust in God becomes your own self-will

to see Him just. And even if for now
His anger does not strike you, you avow
He is not serious with sin. You charge
too many loud words spoken that enlarge

your ego, but they're filled with empty talk.
They are the dust of nothing, and like chalk
will scatter and be lost. What a fool states
is without knowledge, and to naught relates."

JOB: 36

He says that I give vent to nonsense, slurs
that I am but a show of empty words!
And further how the cries of those who call
will go unheeded for three reasons—all

are quite irrelevant if meant for me:
the first, which I disclaim, is vanity,
the second, misdirected and the third,
self-centered. And if I rightly heard

his message, still I shall not interrupt?
Let him continue, though his thought's corrupt.
Thus he went on: "Bear with me yet a while
and I'll instruct you how I will compile

some notes on God's behalf; search far and wide
across the universe to be my guide,
it will support my testimony. First,
God is righteous. This utterance may burst

your mind, but I declare the thought is true.
The perfect One in knowledge is with you.
Behold, too, God is mighty. He'll despise
no one. In strength and wisdom I apprise

how He is perfect. He gives to the poor
both right and honors. The wicked, I'm sure,
find no reward, nor are their lives preserved.
God takes note of the good; He has not swerved

from hearing their just claims. Why, He puts kings
on thrones, establishing forever things
pertaining to their lofty power. For
if they are bound in fetters, even more

fast bound in cords of misery, well then,
God will denounce their conduct to these men.
He'll tell why and what faults precipitate
their fall. If pride, He will elucidate

rebellion, tyranny and insolence.
In opening their ears to their offense,
He'll tell them, too, they must return from wrong.
If they obey and serve, they become strong,

will spend their days in happiness, their years
brimming and filled with pleasures. Oh, what tears
are theirs who will not heed! They'll perish by
the sword and without knowledge will they die.

The godless are those hypocrites of heart
who'll reap His wrath, then find themselves apart.
They cannot cry for help when they're confined,
their souls succumb in youth, their lives resigned

to the shame to which they are addicted.
With affliction God saves the afflicted.
Thus by the discipline of suffering
He speaks into their ear His threatening

rebuke. Out of distress God has enticed
you with prosperity. What has sufficed
to fill the judgment of the wicked? You're
consumed by your own grievances, too poor

to be preoccupied with what is just.
Beware no anger leads to your disgust
nor that you scoff at God and turn aside
into rebellion. Let your grief not hide

that God's the only one to rescue you.
Will He esteem your riches? Or see through
your gold? No, what they claim as power's naught,
even your high position! If you sought

to night, desire not the dark, the time
when nations pass away. Take heed! The climb
of pride is tempting, but turn not to sin
nor choose it for affliction. To begin,

God is exalted by His power. Tell
if you are able, who can teach as well?
Who prescribed His way, or said that He's done
wrong, absurd or evil? Whoever spun

such tales should first reflect and then extol
His work which men see, sing of His control
and fame. Behold how great God is! We know
Him not, the number of His years, how so

to search them out. Eternity to gauge
(though far apart we mortals look), each stage
as of a rising storm. First the small drops
of water God pours down as rain, and stops

not as they distill the mist. Soon the clouds
abundantly drop rain that then enshrouds
the land. At best who understands, who views
His thunder or the lightning that ensues?

How they are spread and scattered as by plan
that punishes or blesses every man!
By acts as mighty, God brings food profuse;
in covering His hands with light, what use

He will command to launch it to its mark?
His anger calls the tempest, strikes it stark,
the noise tells all concerning Him; you'll see,
God storms His wrath against iniquity!"

JOB: 37

In this last chapter of Elihu's speech
he'll now describe God's glory, hope to reach
conclusions that are new and relevant.
And he'll philosophize within the scant

time left, continuing to show as past,
what is the force of nature to contrast
with God's own will. So thus I read his word
and glean the meaning from what I have heard.

The implication is my ignorance,
how to decipher the significance
of these communications that are God's.
I catch the tone implicit that His rods

of lightning bring both anger and relief.
To justify myself, more than belief,
is what I lack and feel somehow is lost.
Yet this does not concern him, at no cost

has he begun to comprehend my plight.
And so the text continues, that despite
its length I listen hopefully to gain
the solace I seek and cannot attain.

"How my heart trembles, wildly leaps its bound,
just as I listen to the thunder-sound
of God's voice! As the storm's roar, so it seems
to peal from heaven, roll by as if streams

across the sky, so is His lightning blaze
to reach the ends of earth. Behind the haze
that roars His thunder of majestic voice,
it's He allows them to be heard. His choice

is glorious! The great things He'll perform,
we can't discern them. He'll say to the storm
or snow or rain, 'Go down to earth, be fierce.'
To stop the work of men's hands, He will pierce

their actions with His wondrous force, so all
will know they're subject to a higher call.
When the tornado blows, wild beasts will sneak
into their lairs and hidden refuge seek.

Then from the south will come the tempest's rain;
out of the north the cold, and in like vein
by God's own very breath will He provide
the frost where widest rivers freeze. He'll guide

the thick cloud loading it with moisture; send
forth lightning, and will scatter it to bend
their bolts to do His will throughout the earth.
He'll see these storms ensuing, and their worth

is for correction, for the land or love,
a curse of mercy, coming from above.
Oh, hearken, Job, and hear this argument:
stand still, consider the whole, vast extent

of all God's wondrous works. Do you know how
or when He has disposed them? You allow
for His commands, but do you realize
what makes light dart out from the clouds? Surmise,

if can you, or fathom the balancing
of His wonderful works, how He can bring
such perfect order, knowledge and such skill
to them! Do you know why your clothes can fill

your body with their warmth when south winds
blow? Can you with God spread out the sky, aglow
so like a molten mirror? Who has taught
you what to say to God? You, who know naught,

will you tell how we can draw near to God?
We cannot know in ignorance; how odd
it would be told to Him what we would say.
And if I speak or dare approach, what way

shall I be and not swallowed up? So men
see not the bright light of the sun again,
riding the crest of clouds high in the sky,
nor know when wind will pass and blow. The eye

can't see the majesty of God break forth
from heaven, clothed with splendor. From the north
fair weather comes, and if we can but touch
the Almighty, can we find Him out? Much

more to the point, we can't imagine part
of God's great power, yet He has a heart!
His excellence in justice is well known
and He will not afflict. He does not own

the least temptation to destroy. This fact,
although beyond the ken of man, He'll act
with fear and uppermost respect. Conceit
does not impress God, nor will He compete."

JOB: 38

Elihu ends his oratory stint
amid a verbiage well aimed to hint
the wonders wrought by God. Who now is left
to reckon or contend with me? The deft

hand of Almighty God? And so the Lord
then answered from the whirlwind, to afford
the most profound yet simple words heard yet—
what here was said I never shall forget.

"Who darkens counsel by his words without
knowledge? Brace yourself when I ask about
some questions to which you'll reply. But first,
where were you when I, when creation burst

upon the earth from My foundations laid?
Tell me so if your understanding's made
you wise. And then, who measured out the earth,
do you know who surveyed and scaled its girth?

How are its structures fastened, who supports
them, or who laid the cornerstone? Retorts
from you? And while the morning stars all sang
together and the angels of God rang

a chorus with their shouts of joy, say who
shut up the sea's portals when it first spew
from the deep bosom of the earth? Who swathed
the brine with garments of clouds and then bathed

it in thick darkness? Tell me who prescribed
its bounds, set bars and doors? Who has described
its shores and said, 'Only thus far you'll come
and no farther,' to the proud wave? Oh, numb

man, have you commanded the morning since
your days began and caused the dawn to wince,
to know its place? Or have you ever taught
the daylight that it may take hold of aught

and grasp the fringes of the earth, and shake
its ends to cease night's wickedness, and make
it changed as clay under a seal? For sure,
objects that hitherto have been obscure

now take form and color—as if they're wrapped
in a clinging garment—so daylight's trapped
the wicked. Soon the dark which acts as light
will disappear to them. As goes the night,

so do they lose their power to bring harm.
And what is broken? Their uplifted arm!
Have you once entered to explore the springs
beneath the seas? Or wondered through the things

the lie upon the bottom of the deep?
Or have the gates of death opened from sleep?
And do you know where they're situated,
or seen, and by whom habituated?

Have you perceived the earth's breath, can you declare
where light comes from, or how one travels there?
Can you place the darkness, to its bound
do you know where its paths lie, where is found

its source? Doubtless you know, for you were born
before creation's birth, before its morn!
Have you entered the treasures of the snow,
or seen where hail is made and stored, or know

what I've reserved against the time I'll need
them as an arsenal of war? Proceed,
if you can tell, how the light gets parted,
or its path of disposal. Who started

the east wind, scattered it upon the world?
Who made a channel for the rain that hurled
its torrents on a thirsty earth? Which way
do lightning and God's thunder go? Or say

who caused the rain to be where none reside,
in desert wilderness, waste ground beside?
And who will cause the bud of herbs to bloom,
until the air is filled with their perfume?

Has the rain a father? And who begot
the drops of dew? Out of whose womb, what spot
comes ice and heaven's hoary frost? As stone
are waters hardened, freezing as they moan

upon the face of ice, whose deep is hid.
These forces of My nature, who amid
the sons of man can undo, be at ease,
with, say, Orion, or bind Pleiades?

The signs of the zodiac, who'll direct
them to bring each season out? Who'll protect
them, or who guides Arcturus and his sons?
(The constellation of the Bear, these ones.)

Who can control the skies, who will proclaim
the rules that govern heaven? Who will name
or can determine nature's laws on earth,
or who can shout at clouds and then give birth

to rain? Or can you make lightning appear,
does it speak humbly to you, 'I am here?'
Or who put wisdom in the inward parts
and who gives understanding to the hearts?

Just say who numbers all the clouds on high,
who stays these skins of heaven? It is I!
For when the dust grows hard I'll tilt a cloud,
and all the clods that cleave fast, who allowed

them to drink drenching rain? Or who will hunt
prey for the lioness, as is her wont,
to satisfy the craving of her young
as they crouch in their dens, or wait among

their jungle haunts? Who gives the raven food
when all its fledglings cry to God: that brood
will wander in hunger, searching for meat;
tell who supplies their mouths something to eat?"

JOB: 39

Inscrutable these words that touch a chord
to echo chastening! So from the Lord
they came not as I questioned fate, but then
a challenge put to me as to all men.

The varied mysteries, the universe,
who can explain these things? Who's so athirst
for knowledge he can know? The list grows long
as God speaks to me—I reflect the strong

presence of God. "Job, can you comprehend
how wild goats of the hills breed? Or pretend
to know or control when the doe will give
birth? Can you know the months the young will live

in the mother's womb till their time is due,
then bring them forth when painful birth is through?
The young grow fast in strength; in open field
they roam, then leave not to return—how sealed

their purpose! And who sets the wild ass free?
Who lets him roam at large in meadows? See,
they have steppes to live in, salt lands to dwell,
for how they hate the city's noise, the yell

of drivers shouting at them. So the range
of mountains is their pasture, where the strange
land keeps each blade of grass. The wild ox, will
he be content to serve you, stay until

the night within his stall? Or can you bind
him to the plow for you when he's of mind
to harrow in the valleys? Can you trust
him, since he's so strong, feeling you must

leave your labor to him? Can you rely
upon him to return and bring your rye
and grain into the threshing floor? How wave
the proud wings of the ostrich? But who gave

the pinions and the plumage? And are these
feathers that attest to mother-love? Please!
She lays her eggs upon the ground, and when
she leaves them on dust to be warmed, why then

she never thinks a foot may crush, nor that
a wild beast trample them. Her habitat
is to deal harshly with the young as though
they were not hers. And she'll ignore them so

that if they die, she's hardened, unconcerned
her labor was in vain. She has not learned
of wisdom, God did not impart to her
the understanding. And yet, I aver

when she'll arouse herself to flight, she'll pass
the swiftest horse, his rider, too. Alas!
And did you give the horse his might? His neck,
did you clothe with thunder his mane? Oh, check

if it were you who made him to fear, leap
as a grasshopper. His snorting will keep
the deaf awake, so terrible its sound.
He paws the valley proudly, and is found

exalting in strength, as he mocks at fear
to rush forward to battle. From the spear,
sword or javelin he'll not run away;
with fierceness and rage he enters the fray,

and cannot stand still when the trumpet blows.
'Aha,' he says, as he smells with his nose
the battle, and its thunder and shouting.
Oh, how he's glad he's part of the routing!

Or is it by your wisdom the hawk soars,
pushing his wings toward the south as he roars
by? Does the eagle rise at your command
to make his nest on high? Because you planned

for him to live among the rocks, he dwells
upon the crags of mountains? And who tells
from whence he seeks his prey, eagerly scan
the distance as he spies his food? Who can

say of his young that suck up blood? The slain,
wherever they are, there he is; in vain
is he found in another place. So serve
these lessons of God's government. Observe!"

JOB: 40

Yet still the Lord continues: in effect
what He is saying is how circumspect
I am to doubt His rule. Am I as wise
as He? If so, and only then, my eyes

can be cast on the universe. And not
until I am as able is one jot
of criticism valid. "Shall he that
contends with God instruct Him? Is this chat

to reprove God? Answer, I pray." And oh,
compelled to speak, the words came in a flow
of self-analysis, for then I said:
"Behold, I am of small account! Misled,

how can I now reply? I'll lay my hand
upon my lips to silence them. How grand
I spoke once! Even twice I answered. Yes,
but I'll proceed no farther, no redress

have I." Then from the whirlwind God replied,
"Gird your loins like a man and I will chide
you and demand an answer. How you dare
deny that I am just! You seem to care

not if you put Me in the wrong if you
only appear right. Is it false or true
yours is an arm like God's? The thunder of
your voice, does it compare? The glow above,

the glory, majesty and excellence
can you array yourself with these? Commence
to do so, cast abroad your rage and let
it overflow against the proud. Forget

not to humiliate the haughty, tread
down the wicked in their place, or instead
just hide them in the dust and bind their face
in death's haunt below. If you can embrace

all these, then I'll agree in turn your right
hand gives you victory. Take the sight
of Behemoth, the hippopotamus
(who of all beasts, his size is enormous),

I made you as I did him who will eat
grass as an ox. See his strong loins replete
with strength in the muscles of his belly.
His tail is straight as cedar; also he

has sinews in his thighs knit together,
and his bones are strong as brass. Whether
you know it or not, his ribs are like bars
of iron. In all the earth, counting stars

(in fact all of creation) none's so fierce
as he. And who would master him must pierce
him with a mighty sword! The mountains all
bring food for him where creatures play 'mid tall

shade trees. Under the lotus plant he lies,
half-hid by the cover of reeds, the guise
of marshes and the willows of a brook
surround him. From the trees, if you will look,

their shadows cover him. And if by chance
the river should be turbulent, no glance
from him, for he is not disturbed by it.
His confidence holds firm. He'll even fit

the Jordan in his mouth, or one as swift
and strong! Who can take him with hooks, or lift
a spear to pierce his nose, or even blind
his eyes? Who takes him off guard, makes him mind?"

JOB: 41

"Or take another of my creatures, scan
the crocodile we'll call Leviathan.
Can you draw this one out with a fishhook,
or press down his tongue with a cord? Or look

and see if it is possible to put
a rope in this beast's nose, or pierce his foot
or jaw with some huge spike? Will he plead with
you softly, begging mercy? That's a myth!

And will he make a covenant to be
your slave for life? Such domesticity
is not for him! Nor can you make a pet
of him, play with him like a bird, nor yet

can leash him for your little girls? Will those
with whom you trade bargain, do you suppose,
to carve him up? Can any fill his hide
with harpoons, his head with fishing spears? I'd

doubt it! Lay your hand on him in battle,
it will be the last you do, and that'll
teach you not to try again! No, the hope
of him is useless who would try with rope

to capture him. In fact, all who will look
on him are frightened at his sight. It took
the bravest, yet no one is quite so wild
to stir his anger up! Who'd be beguiled

to think that he can stand before God then?
Whatever's under heaven is Mine, when
I owe to no one naught! I'll not keep still
concerning his limbs nor his strength, nor will

I be silent about his goodly frame.
Who can strip off his outer garments, name
who penetrates his double coat of mail:
who dares come near his jaws? Ask who will pale

at the sight of his large, terrible teeth,
and tell who can open his mouth! Beneath
his overlapping scales, his pride—a shield
sealed tight together—so no one can wield

an instrument upon it, nor can air
penetrate its armor. Not anywhere
is there a space between them. When he'll sneeze,
how sprays of light are sent forth; they must tease

the sparkle in his eyes to shine as dew.
From his mouth come flaming torches; they spew
their fire as smoke flows from his nose, like
from a seething pot or cauldron. The strike

of his breath can kindle coals, then from his
mouth a flame shoots forth. How truly it is
he whose tremendous strength is in his neck!
See terror dance before him; not a speck

does he display, for how his flesh is hard
and firm, not to be moved. Likewise the guard
that locks his heart, it is as cold as stone.
When he lifts himself up, the mighty own

such fear that terror grips them. They're beside
themselves! The sword may reach him, I confide,
but it cannot contain him—neither dart,
spear, nor pointed shaft of javelin. Part

of his great power lies in how he thinks:
for he esteems iron as straw; he winks
at brass as if it were but rotted wood;
an arrow cannot make him free, and should

slingshots be used against him they'll be turned
to stubble! And clubs, too, so unconcerned
is he, he'll laugh at them and the shaking
of a spear. His belly, no mistaking

it, for that is like scales as sharp as bits
of broken pottery which he drags, it's
plain to see, across the mire. He makes
the deep boil like a pot; at times he breaks

the sea until it churns, leaving behind
a shining wake of froth, as like a kind
of frost. In all the earth there's not his like,
a creature without fear. Were he to strike

at anything that he beholds, all high
and mighty, even they'll know fright. His eye
is over all! He's king to every beast,
and children of pride, they're the very least."

JOB: 42

Against such a recital, who can stand?
The evidence is overwhelming and
convincing that to God alone belong
all wisdom, power, intellect. How wrong

to think I have not learned the folly of
my ways! I see how I can trust His love,
although I do not fully comprehend.
The Judge of all the earth cannot offend!

Here's then my answer to the Lord: "I know
You can do all things and that You bestow
on no one power to withhold a thought.
Your purpose none can thwart, so I have fought

in vain! Say who can hide counsel without
knowledge? I tried, and so I spoke about
wonderful things I cannot know full well.
You said previously that I should tell

the answers to Your questions if I can.
I now reply to You. I've heard that man
hears by the hearing of the ear. As for
me, though, now that I've seen You I abhor

myself and loathe the words I spoke. In dust
and ashes I repent, humbled I must
retract what I have voiced." And it was that,
after the Lord had spoken these words, at

which He turned to Eliphaz and said,
"My wrath is kindled against you who fled
from speaking truthfully as Job has done,
and also against your two friends. Not one

of you said what is right! So I request
all three to pay for how you have transgressed.
Take now seven young bulls and seven rams
and offer a burnt offering. The lambs

you'll give to Job at which time he will pray
for you. It will be up to Me to weigh
if I should deal more harshly seeing how
you've spoken foolishly." My three friends now

did as the Lord commanded them to do.
My prayer was accepted, and when through
then God gave me back twice what I had lost.
All past captivity my dear God tossed

away! Then all my brothers, sisters, friends
arrived to break bread at my house. So ends
my sadness and my trial. And all who came
so comforted me for my prior shame,

and all the evil God brought to my home,
they each brought me a money gift. No tome
need I write here about my joy! Beside
this, they gave me a golden ring; that I'd

such blessings showered on me, counting all
the Lord did, to my latter days befall
more good than when my trial did first commence.
The numbers are of little consequence,

yet I shall note them only to relate
how God repays the faithful who will wait
for Him. Now I have fourteen thousand sheep,
six thousand camels, all for me to keep;

a thousand teams of oxen, donkeys too,
at least a thousand of them. Wouldn't you
be grateful as I was to be restored
this property? But greater than the hoard,

I soon had seven sons, three daughters when
I realized my lesson once again.
The first I named Jemima which can mean
as beautiful as day, or as serene

or as a dove; the next Keziah speaks
as fragrant as the cinnamon; who peeks
to see my third will find her name denote
a horn of plenty: Keren-Happuch. Gloat

on them I must, for they are truly fair,
in fact throughout the land none can compare!
So beautiful my girls, I should make clear
I put them in my will! I volunteer

such information that you realize
this joyous ending; to idealize
my whole experience may be of worth.
Said simply it resorts to this: no dearth

of meaningful conclusion here. I asked
a question, and the answer was not masked
but found in God Himself. So it evolved
and my reward is that I am absolved.

Poetic justice? Never, not the word,
not even what I thought nor what I heard.
The vital element beyond what haps
is that I saw God face-to-face. The traps

the intellectual will find, are those
that would reconcile, not the things I chose
to think this lesson is about, but these
which all my friends pursued. And if you please,

what I have also come to see as truth:
human incompetence! It takes no sleuth
to see how the reverse is also just.
Divine omnipotence! This says I must

confess the whole, broad lesson I have learned,
a lecture to pass on, so dearly earned.
And after this, as one counts fleeting time,
I lived one hundred forty years and I'm

rewarded to be satisfied of days,
to see four generations and the ways
of all my sons. So much for history
and what occurred, as in a dream to me:

what took me past the tragedy of life
to find how we are rooted beyond strife,
and forces us to meet God, to commune
and with him. Alas, we pass this way too soon!

THE END

ABOUT THE AUTHOR

ANITA H. ROSENAU was born in Philadelphia, the only child of Anna and Joseph Halpern. She wrote her first play in sixth grade, and her first published poem was in an anthology of poetry by college students when she was a freshman in the University of Pennsylvania. As an honors major in Economics, her interest was in business; however in 1944, when she graduated, women were not granted degrees from the Wharton School. Her degree, therefore, was in Liberal Arts from the College for Women. Upon graduation she worked briefly for the War Labor Board in Philadelphia as a Junior Economist.

After marriage to Gary Rosenau and having two children, Gail and Gareth, Rosenau went back to college and received her Master of Arts degree from Temple University in Philadelphia. Because of her love for playwriting, her major was Theatre. It took her two years to convince the University to let her write a creative thesis for her degree, thus becoming the first person in the history of the University to do so. She wrote an original trilogy in blank verse, "Lancelot and Guinevere."

Because of a deep love for the Bible, which is part of a daily study routine, Rosenau took the story of Ruth from the four chapters in the Bible and wrote Ruth's story in first person in verse. This was published as a cassette, with Rosenau narrating.

The idea of Bible characters telling their story in this form became something she decided to pursue. The story of Joseph was written for older children, the story of Moses was designed for young children, and then a more scholarly approach was taken for the stories of David and Job.

"Guinevere," the third play in the trilogy "Lancelot and Guinevere," became the libretto for an opera. Although that opera was never finished, part of it was performed at the Wheeler Opera House in Aspen, at Lincoln Center in New York, and it had its European premier at the Dubrovnic Music Festival.

There have been a number of staged readings of Rosenau's plays off-Broadway and in diverse venues in Colorado. A reading of her one-woman play, "A Woman of Purpose," was sponsored by the Aspen Art Museum which also sponsored "Islands," the second play in a modern trilogy including "Strangers." A reading of that play was sponsored by the University of Denver as part of the Aspen Playwright's Conference.

Many of Rosenau's poems have been published. Her poem "Prayer to God" is published in the anthology of poetry "Ideas on Wings," the only anthology of poetry ever published by the Christian Science Publishing Society.